UPDATED +
EXPANDED

THE
FIRST
90
DAYS

Proven Strategies *for* Getting Up *to* Speed Faster *and* Smarter

MICHAEL D. WATKINS

Harvard Business Review Press • Boston, Massachusetts

Copyright 2013 Michael D. Watkins

All rights reserved
Printed in the United States of America
26 25 24 23 22

The First 90 Days®, Acceleration Coaching™, Rapid Rewire™, Transition
Roadmap™, Transition Risk Assessment™, and Transition Heat Map™ are
trademarks of Genesis Advisers.

No part of this publication may be reproduced, stored in or introduced into
a retrieval system, or transmitted, in any form, or by any means (electronic,
mechanical, photocopying, recording, or otherwise), without the prior
permission of the publisher. Requests for permission should be directed to
permissions@hbsp.harvard.edu, or mailed to Permissions, Harvard Business
School Publishing, 60 Harvard Way, Boston, Massachusetts 02163.

The web addresses referenced in this book were live and correct at the time of
the book's publication but may be subject to change.

Library of Congress Cataloging-in-Publication Data

Watkins, Michael, 1956-
  The first 90 days : proven strategies for getting up to speed faster and smarter /
Michael Watkins. ---[Updated and expanded edition].
    pages cm
  ISBN 978-1-4221-8861-3 (hardback)
  1. Leadership. 2. Executive ability. 3. Strategic planning. 4. Management.
I. Title. II. Title: First ninety days.
  HD57.7.W38 2013
  658.4 --- dc23

                          2012047185

The paper used in this publication meets the requirements of the American
National Standard for Permanence of Paper for Publications and Documents in
Libraries and Archives Z39.48-1992.

To Aidan,

Maeve, and Niall

My beautiful children.

—M. W.

CONTENTS

Preface for the 10th Anniversary Edition   *xi*

Introduction: The First 90 Days   1

Why transitions are critical times. How new leaders can
take charge more effectively. Building career transition
competence. Assessing transition risk in taking a new role.

1. Prepare Yourself   19

Why people fail to make the mental break from their old
jobs. Preparing to take charge in a new role. Understanding
the challenges of promotion and onboarding. Assessing
preferences and vulnerabilities.

2. Accelerate Your Learning   45

Learning as an investment process. Planning to learn.
Figuring out the best sources of insight. Using structured
methods to accelerate learning.

3. Match Strategy to Situation   69

The dangers of "one-best-way" thinking. Diagnosing
the situation to develop the right strategy. The STARS
model of types of transitions. Using the model to analyze
portfolios and lead change.

4. Negotiate Success   87

Building a productive working relationship with a new boss.
The five-conversations framework. Defining expectations.
Agreeing on a diagnosis of the situation. Figuring out
how to work together. Negotiating for resources. Putting
together your 90-day plan.

5. Secure Early Wins   115

Avoiding common traps. Figuring out A-item priorities.
Creating a compelling vision. Building personal credibility.
Getting started on improving organizational performance.
Plan-then-implement change versus collective learning.

6. Achieve Alignment   139

The role of the leader as organizational architect.
Identifying the root causes of poor performance. Aligning
strategy, structure, systems, skills, and culture.

7. Build Your Team   165

Inheriting a team and changing it. Managing the tension
between short-term and long-term goals. Working team
restructuring and organizational architecture issues in
parallel. Putting in place new team processes.

8. Create Alliances   199

The trap of thinking that authority is enough. Identifying
whose support is critical. Mapping networks of influence
and patterns of deference. Altering perceptions of interests
and alternatives.

9. Manage Yourself 221

How leaders get caught in vicious cycles. The three pillars of self-efficacy. Creating and enforcing personal disciplines. Building an advice-and-counsel network.

10. Accelerate Everyone 239

Why so few companies focus on transition acceleration. The opportunity to institutionalize a common framework. Using the framework to accelerate team development, develop high-potential leaders, integrate acquisitions, and strengthen succession planning.

Notes 259
Index 265
About the Author 279

PREFACE FOR THE 10TH ANNIVERSARY EDITION

What a difference a decade makes. When I set out to write *The First 90 Days* in 2001, little was out there about getting up to speed in new roles or onboarding new hires (hereafter "leadership transitions").[1] At the time, I was teaching negotiation and corporate diplomacy at Harvard Business School. Although I had coauthored a modestly successful book on senior executive transitions in 1999—*Right from the Start* with Dan Ciampa—I had been counseled by my colleagues at HBS that it was a risky career move to focus further on the subject.[2]

While I appreciated their advice, in the end I decided to push forward to write the book. Leadership transitions were just too interesting and ripe for study; it was virtually an untilled field from both intellectual and practical points of view. Also in late 1999, soon after the publication of *Right from the Start*, I had been asked by Johnson & Johnson's corporate management development group to develop workshops and coaching processes to accelerate the company's leaders in transition. This work soon evolved into an engaging development partnership, and J&J became a test bed for the development and deployment of my ideas.

The First 90 Days was a distillation of what I had learned during roughly two and a half years of working with hundreds of leaders at the vice president and director levels in all regions of the world. The book built on some foundational ideas developed in *Right from the Start*; for example the importance of accelerating learning, securing early wins, and creating alliances. However, the ideas had been augmented, tested, modified, and turned into practical frameworks and tools for helping leaders at all levels accelerate their transitions.

It was that distillation—the mix of concepts, tools, cases, and practical advice—that really hit the mark with leaders in transition. I had the wonderful experience of seeing sales of *The First 90 Days*, which was published in November 2003, take off like a rocket. By the summer of 2004, the book was on the *Business Week* best-seller list; it stayed there for fifteen months. This success coincided fortuitously with my departure from Harvard and fueled my decision not to seek another academic position. Instead I cofounded a leadership development company—Genesis Advisers—dedicated to helping companies accelerate everyone taking new roles.

Business books, even highly successful ones, tend to sell strongly for a year or two and then fade. This has not been the case for *The First 90 Days*. I have had the pleasure of seeing the book sell strongly for a decade, having so far sold almost eight hundred thousand copies in English, including seventy-five thousand in 2011. For the past ten years, the book has consistently remained among Harvard Business Review Press's best-sellers. It has also been translated into twenty-seven languages and was the basis for *Leadership Transitions*, Harvard Business Publishing's award-winning e-learning tool.[3]

Enduring success of this kind has qualified *The First 90 Days* to be labeled a "business classic." The term "classic" evokes a whiff of mustiness with which I am not entirely comfortable.

Nonetheless, I was honored in 2009 to have the book named one of the 100 best business books of all time after an extensive review by Jack Covert and Todd Sattersten at 800-CEO-READ. That recognition was a mark not only of the importance and staying power of the ideas, but also of the continuing need for every new generation of leaders to learn to make successful transitions.

The success of *The First 90 Days* also fueled and was fueled by a rising wave of interest on the part of companies in talent management, onboarding of new hires, and CEO succession. From the outset, Genesis Advisers' work at J&J focused on both accelerating new hires and speeding up internal promotions; I continue to believe that it is a mistake to focus just on onboarding and not on accelerating all transitions. However, it was interest in onboarding that really propelled the field forward, as the war for talent became ever more fierce, and the high costs of derailment, under-performance, and lack of retention of new hires more evident. So many companies began to adopt First 90 Days ideas to accelerate onboarding of new hires. Beyond the work we have done with our clients at Genesis Advisers, First 90 Days concepts and tools have independently been adapted and implemented by learning and development and human resources professionals in thousands of companies. In 2006 *The Economist* named *The First 90 Days* "the onboarding bible."[4] More recently, the increasing maturity of the field has been marked by major conferences devoted to the subject of onboarding and transition acceleration.

My own thinking, of course, has also evolved over the past decade, and this has resulted in numerous improvements in this new edition of the book. I have remained deeply engaged in working with leaders in transition, doing research, and translating my practical experience and findings into better frameworks and tools. Key follow-on publications include:

- *Shaping the Game*, a 2006 Harvard Business Review Press book that looks at how new leaders should apply ideas from the fields of negotiation and influence to make successful transitions.[5]

- *The First 90 Days in Government*, a version of *The First 90 Days* adapted to the public sector and coauthored with Peter Daly, a retired senior Treasury Department official, and Cate Reavis.[6]

- "The Pillars of Executive Onboarding," an October 2008 *Talent Management* article on the major focal points for onboarding: business orientation, expectations, alignment, cultural adaptation, and political connection.[7]

- *Your Next Move*, a 2009 Harvard Business Press book that highlights the need for leaders in transition to distinguish between the organizational change challenges and the personal adaptive challenges they are confronting. It also takes a deep dive into specific types of transitions such as promotion, leading former peers, onboarding, and international moves.[8]

- "Picking the Right Transition Strategy," a January 2009 *Harvard Business Review* article that further develops the STARS framework (start-up, turnaround, accelerated growth, realignment, and sustaining success) introduced in the first edition of *The First 90 Days* for matching transition strategy to these various types of business situations.[9]

- "How Managers Become Leaders," a June 2012 *Harvard Business Review* article summarizing the research I did on "the seven seismic shifts" that leaders experience as they make the very challenging transition from a senior functional role to running an entire business.[10]

My thinking has also been powerfully informed by my work during the past eight years in developing successive generations of First 90 Days offerings for our clients at Genesis Advisers. Recently this has included a new generation of Acceleration Coaching process, a web-based workshop that includes virtual breakout groups, and a specialized program to help physicians transition from clinical practices and research institutions into commercial environments.

I also have been gratified that *The First 90 Days*, and my subsequent work, have spawned so much interest in the study and practical application of transition acceleration ideas. Much excellent original research and writing has been done.[11] And, since imitation truly is the sincerest form of flattery, I have been flattered to see many of my concepts, tools, and terms adopted by other practitioners and consultants—for example, the STARS framework, transition traps, the importance of securing early wins,[12] the idea of "the fuzzy front-end" (referring to the period between getting a job and formally stepping into the role and developed jointly with Dan Ciampa),[13] and the important distinction between the organizational change challenge and the personal adaptive challenge in assessing the transition risk confronting new leaders.[14]

The past ten years have been a wonderful journey, and I have many people to thank for helping to make it happen. Foremost are the two people who had the biggest impact on the early development of my ideas and their application in the real world: my *Right from the Start* coauthor Dan Ciampa and my partner

Shawna Slack. Then there have been my editors and publishers at Harvard Business Review Press, especially Jeff Kehoe, who has been consistently wonderful in encouraging, directing, and refining my work. I also very much appreciate the support of leaders at key Genesis Advisers client companies who have been willing to take the leap and invest in our work, notably Becky Atkeison and her colleagues at FedEx and Inaki Bastarrika, Ron Bossert, Carolynn Cameron, Michael Ehret, Ted Nguyen, and Doug Soo Hoo at Johnson & Johnson. Finally, my heartfelt gratitude goes to the staff at Genesis Advisers for all their hard work, and especially to Kerry Brunelle for her support in editing the manuscript.

THE FIRST 90 DAYS

Introduction:
The First 90 Days

The president of the United States gets 100 days to prove himself; you get 90. The actions you take during your first few months in a new role will largely determine whether you succeed or fail.

Failure in a new assignment can spell the end of a promising career. But making a successful transition is about more than just avoiding failure. When leaders derail, their problems can almost always be traced to vicious cycles that developed in the first few months on the job. And for every leader who fails outright, there are many others who survive but do not realize their full potential. As a result, they lose opportunities to advance their careers and help their organizations thrive.

Why are transitions critical? When I surveyed more than thirteen hundred senior HR leaders, almost 90 percent agreed that "transitions into new roles are the most challenging times in the professional lives of leaders."[1] And nearly three-quarters agreed that "success or failure during the first few months is a strong predictor of overall success or failure in the job." So even though a bad transition does not necessarily doom you to failure, it makes success a lot less likely.

The good news on transitions is that they give you a chance to start afresh and make needed changes in an organization. But transitions are also periods of acute vulnerability, because you lack established working relationships and a detailed understanding of your new role. You're managing under a microscope, subject to a high degree of scrutiny as people around you strive to figure out who you are and what you represent as a leader. Opinions of your effectiveness begin to form surprisingly quickly, and, once formed, they're very hard to change. If you're successful in building credibility and securing early wins, the momentum likely will propel you through the rest of your tenure. But if you dig yourself into a hole early on, you will face an uphill battle from that point forward.

Building Your Career Transition Competence

A long career at a single company (or even two or three companies) is increasingly a thing of the past. Leaders experience many transitions, so the ability to transition quickly and effectively into a new role has become a critical skill. In a study of 580 leaders conducted jointly by Genesis Advisers, *Harvard Business Review*, and the International Institute of Management Development (hereafter the Genesis/HBR/IMD study), respondents reported an average of 18.2 years of professional work experience.[2] The typical leader had been promoted 4.1 times, moved between business functions (such as from sales to marketing) 1.8 times, joined a new company 3.5 times, moved between business units in the same company 1.9 times, and moved geographically 2.2 times. This totals 13.5 major transitions per leader, or one every 1.3 years. As you will learn later, some of these transitions likely happened in parallel. But the implications are clear: every successful career is a series of successful assignments, and every successful assignment is launched with a successful transition.

Beyond these easily identified milestones, leaders also experience many hidden transitions. These transitions occur when there are substantial changes in leaders' roles and responsibilities without corresponding changes in titles. These are common occurrences, often the result of organizational shifts due to rapid growth, restructuring, and acquisition. Hidden transitions can be particularly perilous, because leaders do not always recognize them or give them the attention they deserve. The most dangerous transition can be the one you don't recognize is happening.

Leaders also are impacted by the transitions of many others around them. Each year about a quarter of the managers in a typical *Fortune* 500 company changes jobs.[3] And each leader transition materially impacts the performance of roughly a dozen other people—bosses, peers, direct reports, and other stakeholders.[4] So even if you aren't personally in transition, you likely are having the transitions of others inflicted on you. To see this, think about the other people in your immediate neighborhood who also are in their first 90 days. The number likely will surprise you.

The problem is that even though a lot has been written and discussed about how to be a more effective leader in general, little research and writing addresses how to successfully accelerate through leadership and career transitions. People still go through these all-important career crucibles with little preparation and no reliable knowledge or tools to help them. That's what this book is designed to give you.

Reaching the Break-Even Point

Your goal in every transition is to get as rapidly as possible to the *break-even point*. This is the point at which you have contributed as much value to your new organization as you have consumed from it. As shown in figure I-1, new leaders are net consumers of

FIGURE I-1

The break-even point

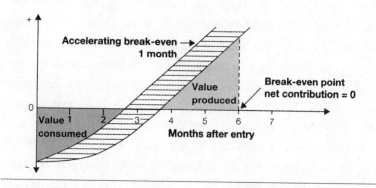

value early on; as they learn and begin to take action, they begin to create value. From the break-even point onward, they are (one hopes) net contributors of value to their organizations.

When more than two hundred company CEOs and presidents were asked for their best estimates of the time it takes a typical midlevel leader who has been promoted or hired from the outside to reach the break-even point, the average of their responses was 6.2 months.[5] Of course, there can be a great deal of variation in the time it takes to reach the break-even point. If you have inherited a disaster—the classic *burning platform*—you may be creating value from the moment your appointment is announced. If you have been hired from the outside into a very successful organization, it may take a year or more for you to be a net value contributor. However, even though the time varies (and I explore in depth the challenges of different types of transitions), the goal is the same: to get there as quickly and effectively as possible.

This book provides a blueprint for dramatically condensing the time it takes you to reach the break-even point, regardless of your level in your organization. In fact, independent research has shown that you can reduce the time by as much as 40 percent through rigorous application of the principles described in this book.[6]

Avoiding Transition Traps

Like most leaders, you've probably learned to make transitions in the school of hard knocks—trying things, making mistakes, and ultimately winning through. In the process, you've developed approaches that have worked for you . . . at least until now. But what works well in some situations doesn't work in others, and you may not figure that out until it's too late. That's why it is crucial to follow a comprehensive framework for making transitions, one that distills the experience of many leaders facing a diverse range of situations.

Consider, for example, the following list of common traps, developed through interviews with experienced leaders and supplemented by responses to questions in the Genesis/HBR/IMD study. As you look at the list, think about your own experience.

Sticking with what you know. You believe you will be successful in the new role by doing the same things you did in your previous role, only more so. You fail to see that success in the new role requires you to stop doing some things and to embrace new competencies.

Falling prey to the "action imperative." You feel as if you need to take action, and you try too hard, too early to put your own stamp on the organization. You are too busy to learn, and you make bad decisions and catalyze resistance to your initiatives.

Setting unrealistic expectations. You don't negotiate your mandate or establish clear, achievable objectives. You may perform well but still fail to meet the expectations of your boss and other key stakeholders.

Attempting to do too much. You rush off in all directions, launching multiple initiatives in the hope that some will pay off. People become confused, and no critical mass of resources gets focused on key initiatives.

Coming in with "the" answer. You come in with your mind made up, or you reach conclusions too quickly about "the" problems and "the" solutions. You alienate people who could help you understand what's going on, and you squander opportunities to develop support for good solutions.

Engaging in the wrong type of learning. You spend too much time focused on learning about the technical part of the business and not enough about the cultural and political dimensions of your new role. You don't build the cultural insight, relationships, and information conduits you need if you're to understand what is really going on.

Neglecting horizontal relationships. You spend too much time focused on vertical relationships—up to the boss and down to direct reports—and not enough on peers and other stakeholders. You don't fully understand what it will take to succeed, and you miss early opportunities to build supportive alliances.

Have you fallen into any of these traps in the past? Have you seen others do so? Now think about your new role. Are you in danger of making any of these mistakes? To help avoid derailment and get to the break-even point faster, keep these in mind as you take on your new role.

Creating Momentum

Each of these traps enmeshes its victims in a *vicious cycle* (see figure I-2). By failing to learn the right things in the right ways at the outset, for example, you can make bad initial decisions that damage your credibility. Then, because people don't trust your judgment, it can become still more difficult to learn what you need to know. You consume energy compensating for early miscalculations, and the downward spiral takes hold.

But your objective is not only to avoid vicious cycles; you need to create *virtuous cycles* that help you create momentum and establish an upward spiral of increasing effectiveness (see figure I-3).

FIGURE I-2

The vicious cycle of transitions

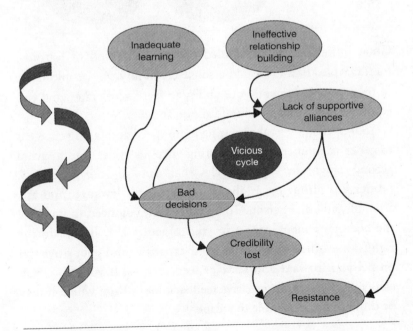

FIGURE I-3

The virtuous cycle of transitions

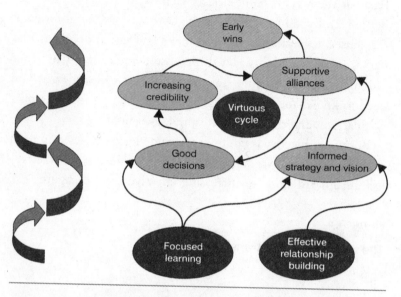

Good initial decisions founded on the right kind of learning, for example, bolster your personal credibility. As people come to trust your judgment, your ability to learn accelerates, and you equip yourself to make sound calls on tougher issues.

Your overriding goal in getting up to speed and taking charge is to generate momentum by creating virtuous cycles, and to avoid getting caught in vicious cycles that damage your credibility. Leadership ultimately is about influence and leverage. You are, after all, only one person. To be successful, you need to mobilize the energy of many others in your organization. If you do the right things, then your vision, your expertise, and your drive can propel you forward and serve as seed crystals. If you don't, you can end up caught in negative feedback loops from which it may be difficult or impossible to escape.

Understanding the Fundamental Principles

The root causes of transition failure always lie in a pernicious interaction between the new role, with its opportunities and pitfalls, and the individual, with his strengths and vulnerabilities. Failure is never only about the flaws of the new leader. Indeed, all the failed leaders I studied had achieved significant successes in the past. Nor is it only about a no-win situation in which not even a superhuman leader could have carried the day. The business situations facing leaders who derail are no tougher than those in which others succeed brilliantly. Transition failures happen because new leaders either misunderstand the essential demands of the situation or lack the skill and flexibility to adapt to them.

The good news is that there are systematic methods you can employ to both lessen the likelihood of failure and reach the break-even point faster. The specific business situations that confront transitioning leaders vary. But specific types of transition situations, such as start-ups and turnarounds, share certain features and imperatives. Further, there are fundamental principles—for example, securing early wins—that underpin success in all transitions at all levels. The key, then, is to match your strategy to the situation.

More than a decade's worth of research and practice has shown that you can dramatically accelerate your transition into your new role. Do the right things—the essential transition tasks listed next—and you will rapidly create momentum that will propel you to even greater successes.

- **Prepare yourself.** This means making a mental break from your old job and preparing to take charge in the new one. Perhaps the biggest pitfall you face is assuming that what has made you successful to this point will continue to do so. The dangers of sticking with what you know, working extremely hard at doing it, and failing miserably are very real.

- **Accelerate your learning.** You need to climb the learning curve as fast as you can in your new organization. This means understanding its markets, products, technologies, systems, and structures, as well as its culture and politics. Learning about a new organization can feel like drinking from a fire hose. You must be systematic and focused about deciding what you need to learn and how you will learn it most efficiently.

- **Match your strategy to the situation.** Different types of situations require you to make significant adjustments in how you plan for and execute your transition. Start-ups, for instance—of a new product, process, plant, or business—present challenges quite different from those you would face while turning around a product, process, or plant in serious trouble. A clear diagnosis of the situation is an essential prerequisite for developing your action plan.

- **Secure early wins.** Early wins build your credibility and create momentum. They create virtuous cycles that leverage the energy you put into the organization to create a pervasive sense that good things are happening. In the first few weeks, you need to identify opportunities to build personal credibility. In the first 90 days, you need to identify ways to create value and improve business results that will help you get to the break-even point more rapidly.

- **Negotiate success.** Because no other single relationship is more important, you need to figure out how to build a productive working relationship with your new boss (or bosses) and manage her expectations. This means carefully planning for a series of critical conversations about the situation, expectations, working style, resources, and your personal development. Crucially, it means developing and gaining consensus on your 90-day plan.

- **Achieve alignment.** The higher you rise in an organization, the more you must play the role of organizational architect. This means figuring out whether the organization's strategic direction is sound, bringing its structure into alignment with its strategy, and developing the processes and skill bases necessary to realize your strategic intent.

- **Build your team.** If you are inheriting a team, you need to evaluate, align, and mobilize its members. You likely also need to restructure it to better meet the demands of the situation. Your willingness to make tough early personnel calls and your capacity to select the right people for the right positions are among the most important drivers of success during your transition and beyond. You need to be both systematic and strategic in approaching the team-building challenge.

- **Create coalitions.** Your success depends on your ability to influence people outside your direct line of control. Supportive alliances, both internal and external, are necessary if you are to achieve your goals. You therefore should start right away to identify those whose support is essential for your success, and to figure out how to line them up on your side.

- **Keep your balance.** In the personal and professional tumult of a transition, you must work hard to maintain your equilibrium and preserve your ability to make good judgments. The risks of losing perspective, becoming isolated, and making bad calls are ever present during transitions. There is much you can do to accelerate your personal transition and to gain more control over your work environment. The right advice-and-counsel network is an indispensable resource.

- **Accelerate everyone.** Finally, you need to help all those in your organization—direct reports, bosses, and peers— accelerate their own transitions. The fact that you're in transition means they are too. The quicker you can get your new direct reports up to speed, the more you will help your own performance. Beyond that, the potential benefits to the organization of systematically accelerating everyone's transitions are vast.

The chapters that follow offer instructive stories and action-able guidelines and tools for succeeding in each of these ten tasks. You will learn how to diagnose your situation and create action plans tailored to your needs, regardless of your level in the orga-nization or the business situation you face. In the process you will build a 90-day plan that will accelerate you into your new role.

Assessing Transition Risk

The first step is to diagnose the types of transitions you're going through. Whether you're preparing to interview for a new position or have taken a new role, this is the starting point for applying the fundamental principles. Promotion and onboarding into new companies are the most frequent shifts.

However, most leaders taking new roles experience multiple transitions in parallel—for example, joining a new company and moving to a new location, or being promoted and moving from a functional to a cross-functional role. In fact, participants in the executive programs we studied reported on average experiencing 2.2 major shifts (such as getting a promotion, joining a new company, moving between business units, moving geographically) the last time they took new roles.[7]

This complexity adds to the transition challenge—and the risk of derailing—and it means it is critical for you to understand the types of transitions you're experiencing and to identify which shifts you are finding most challenging. A simple way to do this is to complete the Transition Risk Assessment in table I-1.

Mapping Out Your First 90 Days

Your transition begins the moment you learn you are being considered for a new job (see figure I-4 for key transition milestones). When it ends depends very much on the situation you face. No matter what kind of transition you're making, by roughly the three-month mark key people in the organization—your bosses, peers, and direct reports—typically expect you to be getting some traction.

Thus, you should use the 90-day period as a planning horizon. Doing so will help you confront the need to operate in a compressed time frame. If you're lucky, you may get some lead time between learning you're being considered and actually sitting in the chair. Use that time to begin educating yourself about your organization.

No matter how much preparation time you get, start planning what you hope to accomplish by specific milestones. Even a few

TABLE I-1

Transition Risk Assessment

To transition effectively, first identify the risks you face as you move into your new role using the Transition Risk Assessment. Start by checking off the types of transitions you are experiencing using the middle column. Then, for each item you checked, assess how challenging you are finding that particular shift on a 1–10 scale, where 1 means very easy and 10 means very difficult. Total the numbers in the right-hand column to get your Transition Risk Index (up to 100). The index gives you a sense of the magnitude of the challenge and the specific dimensions of your overall transition on which you most need to focus.

Type of transition	Check each that applies	Assess relative difficulty for you (1–10)
Moving to a new industry or profession		
Joining a new company		
Moving to a new unit or group in the same company		
Being promoted to a higher level		
Leading former peers (assuming you have been promoted)		
Moving from one function to another (e.g., sales to marketing)		
Taking on a cross-functional leadership role for the first time		
Moving geographically		
Entering a new national or ethnic culture		
Having to do two jobs at the same time (finishing old role while starting new one)		
Taking on a newly created role (as opposed to an existing role)		
Entering an organization in which major change already is going on		
Sum the numbers in the right-most column to calculate your Transition Risk Index		

FIGURE I-4

Key transition milestones

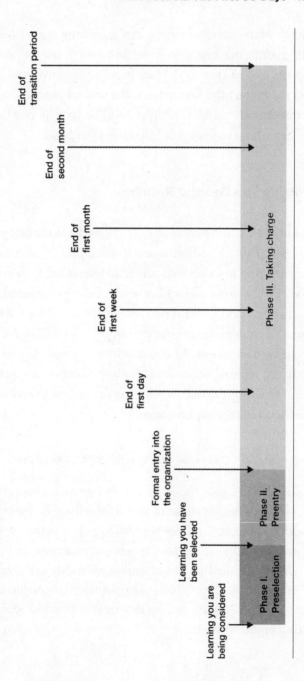

hours of preentry planning can go a long way. Begin by thinking about your first day in the new job. What do you want to do by the end of that day? Then move to the first week. Then focus on the end of the first month, the second month, and finally the three-month mark. These plans will be sketchy, but the simple act of beginning to plan will help clear your head.

Hitting the Ground Running

This book is for new leaders at all levels, from first-time managers to CEOs. The fundamental principles of effective transition acceleration hold up well across all levels. Every new leader needs to quickly become familiar with the new organization, secure early wins, and build supportive coalitions. That's why this book provides guidelines for translating principles into plans tailored to your own situation. As you continue through it, you should read actively, making notes about the applicability of specific points to your situation, as well as thinking about how the advice should be customized to your situation.

Acceleration Checklist and the First 90 Days App

Lists like this one appear at the end of each chapter to help you crystallize the key lessons and apply them to your situation—both to prepare for interviews when you're being considered for a new role and to speed your transition once you are in it.

More detailed guidance and suggestions are provided in the First 90 Days App, which is available in the Apple and Android app store. The app provides day-by-day tips and tools for accelerating your transition.

1. What will it take for you to reach the break-even point more quickly?

2. What are some traps you might encounter, and how can you avoid them?

3. What can you do to create virtuous cycles and build momentum in your new role?

4. What types of transitions are you experiencing? Which are you finding most challenging, and why?

5. What are the key elements and milestones in your 90-day plan?

CHAPTER 1

Prepare Yourself

After eight years in marketing at a leading consumer electronics company, Julia Gould was promoted to lead a major new product development project. Up to that point, her track record had been stellar. Her intelligence, focus, and determination had won her recognition and early promotion to increasingly senior positions. The company had designated her as a high-potential and had positioned her on the fast track to senior leadership.

Julia was assigned to be the launch manager for one of the company's hottest new products. It was her responsibility to coordinate the work of a cross-functional team drawn from marketing, sales, R&D, and manufacturing. The goal: to seamlessly move the product from R&D to production, oversee a rapid ramp-up, and streamline the market introduction.

Unfortunately, Julia ran into trouble early on. Her earlier success in marketing was the result of extraordinary attention to detail. Accustomed to managing with authority and making the calls, she had a high need for control and a tendency to micromanage. When she tried to continue making decisions, members of the team initially said nothing. But soon two key members challenged her knowledge and authority. Stung, she focused on the area she knew best: the marketing aspects of the launch. Her efforts to micromanage the members of the marketing team alienated them. Within a month and a half, Julia was back in marketing, and someone else was leading the team.

Julia failed because she did not make the leap from being a strong functional performer to taking on a cross-functional, project-leadership role. She failed to grasp that the strengths that had made her successful in marketing could be liabilities in a role that required her to lead without direct authority or superior expertise. She kept doing what she knew how to do, making her feel confident and in control. The result, of course, was the opposite. By not letting go of the past and not fully embracing her new role, she squandered a big opportunity to rise in the organization.

It's a mistake to believe that you will be successful in your new job by continuing to do what you did in your previous job, only more so. "They put me in the job because of my skills and accomplishments," the reasoning goes. "So that must be what they expect me to do here." This thinking is destructive, because doing what you know how to do (and avoiding what you don't) can appear to work, at least for a while. You can exist in a state of denial, believing that because you're being efficient, you're being effective. You may keep believing this until the moment the walls come crashing down around you.

What might Julia have done differently? She should have focused on better preparing herself for the new position. At the broadest level, preparing yourself means letting go of the past and embracing the imperatives of the new situation to give yourself a running start. It can be hard work, but it is essential. Often, promising managers fail in new roles because they've failed to prepare themselves by embracing the necessary changes in perspective.

The starting point for preparing yourself is to understand the types of transitions you're experiencing. To illustrate the challenges associated with different types of transitions (discussed in the introduction), I focus here on the two most frequently experienced types of transitions: promotions and onboarding into new companies.

Getting Promoted

A promotion marks the result of years of hard work to persuade influential people in the organization that you're willing and able to move to the next level. But it also marks the beginning of a new journey. You must figure out what it takes to be excellent in the new role, how to exceed the expectations of those who promoted you, and how to position yourself for still greater things. Specifically, every promotion presents new leaders with a core set of challenges to be surmounted.

Balance Breadth and Depth

Each time you're promoted, your horizon broadens to encompass a wider set of issues and decisions. So you need to gain and sustain a high-level perspective in your new role. To be successful, Julia needed to shift her focus from her marketing function to the full array of issues relating to the product launch.

You also need to learn to strike the right balance between keeping the wide view and drilling down into the details. This juggling act can be challenging, because what had been the fifty-thousand-foot view in your previous role may be equivalent to the world at five thousand feet, or even five hundred feet, in your new job.

Rethink What You Delegate

The complexity and ambiguity of the issues you are dealing with increase every time you get promoted. So you'll need to rethink what you delegate. No matter where you land, the keys to effective delegation remain much the same: you build a team of competent people whom you trust, you establish goals and metrics to monitor their progress, you translate higher-level goals into specific responsibilities for your direct reports, and you reinforce them through process.

When you get promoted, however, what you delegate usually needs to change. If you're leading an organization of five people, it may make sense to delegate specific tasks such as drafting a piece of marketing material or selling to a particular customer. In an organization of fifty people, your focus may shift from tasks to projects and processes. At five hundred people, you often need to delegate responsibility for specific products or platforms. And at five thousand people, your direct reports may be responsible for entire businesses.

Influence Differently

Conventional wisdom says that the higher you go, the easier it is to get things done. Not necessarily. Paradoxically, when you get promoted, positional authority often becomes less important for pushing agendas forward. Like Julia, you may indeed gain increased scope to influence decisions that affect the business, but the way you need to engage may be quite different. Decision making becomes more political—less about authority, and more about influence. That isn't good or bad; it's simply inevitable.

There are two major reasons this is so. First, the issues you're dealing with become much more complex and ambiguous when you move up a level—and your ability to identify "right" answers based solely on data and analysis declines correspondingly. Decisions are shaped more by others' expert judgments and who trusts whom, as well as by networks of mutual support.

Second, at a higher level of the organization, the other players are more capable and have stronger egos. Remember, you were promoted because you are able and driven; the same is true for everyone around you. So it shouldn't come as a surprise that the decision-making game becomes much more bruising and politically charged the higher up you go. It's critical, then, for you to become more effective at building and sustaining alliances.

Communicate More Formally

The good news about moving up is that you get a broader view of the business and more latitude to shape it. The bad news is that you are farther from the front lines and more likely to receive filtered information. To avoid this, you need to establish new communication channels to stay connected with what is happening where the action is. You might maintain regular, direct contact with select customers, for instance, or meet regularly with groups of frontline employees, all without undermining the integrity of the chain of command.

You also need to establish new channels for communicating your strategic intent and vision across the organization—convening town-hall–type meetings rather than individual or small-group sessions, or using electronic communication to broadcast your messages to the widest possible audiences. Your direct reports should play a greater role in communicating your vision and ensuring the spread of critical information—something to remember when you're evaluating the leadership skills of the team members you've inherited.

Exhibit the Right Presence

"All the world's a stage," as William Shakespeare put it in the play *As You Like It*, "and all the men and women merely players." One inescapable reality of promotion is that you attract much more attention and a higher level of scrutiny than before. You become the lead actor in a crucial public play. Private moments become fewer, and there is mounting pressure to exhibit the right kind of leadership presence at all times.

That's why it's important to get an early fix on what "leadership presence" means in your new role: what does a leader look like at your new level in the hierarchy? How does he act? What kind of personal leadership brand do you want to have in the new role? How will you make it your own? These are critical considerations, worth taking the time to explore.

These core promotion challenges are summarized in figure 1-1.

Onboarding into a New Company

In promotion situations, leaders typically understand a lot about their organizations but must develop the behaviors and competencies required to be effective at new levels. If you've been hired into a new organization, you will confront very different transition challenges. Leaders joining new companies often are making lateral moves: they've been hired to do things that they've been successful doing elsewhere. Their difficulties lie in adjusting

FIGURE 1-1

Core promotion challenges

For each core challenge there are corresponding strategies that newly promoted leaders should employ.

What's really changed?	What should you do?
Broader impact horizon. There is a broader range of issues, people, and ideas to focus on.	Balance depth and breadth.
Greater complexity and ambiguity. There are more variables, and there is greater uncertainty about outcomes.	Delegate more deeply.
Tougher organizational politics. There are more powerful stakeholders to contend with.	Influence differently.
Further from the front lines. There is greater distance between you and the people executing on the ground, potentially weakening communication and adding more filters.	Communicate more formally.
More scrutiny. There is more attention paid to your actions by more people, more frequently.	Adjust to greater visibility.

to new organizational contexts that have different political structures and cultures.

To illustrate, consider the experience of David Jones at Energix, a small, rapidly growing wind energy company. David was recruited from a highly regarded global manufacturing firm. An engineer by training, David had risen steadily through the ranks in R&D to become vice president of new-product development for the company's electrical distribution division. David learned to lead in a company that was renowned for its leadership bench strength. The culture leaned toward a command-and-control style of leadership, but people were still expected to speak their minds—and did. The company had long been a leader in the adoption and refinement of process-management methodologies, including total quality management, lean manufacturing, and six sigma.

As the new head of R&D at Energix, David entered a company that had weathered the typical start-up transitions—going from two people to two hundred to two thousand—and was now poised to become a major corporation. As a result, the CEO had told David more than once during the recruiting process that things had to change. "We need to become more disciplined," the chief executive had said. "We've succeeded by staying focused and working as a team. We know each other, we trust each other, and we've come a long way together. But we need to be more systematic in how we do things, or we won't be able to capitalize on and sustain our new size." So David understood that his first major task would be to identify, systematize, and improve the core processes of the R&D organization—an essential first step in laying the foundation for sustained growth.

David dug into the new job with his usual gusto. What he found was a company that had been run largely by the seat of its collective pants. Many important operational and financial processes were not well established; others weren't sufficiently controlled. In new-product development alone, dozens of projects had inadequate specifications or insufficiently precise milestones and deliverables. One critical project, Energix's next-generation large turbine, was nearly a year behind schedule and way over budget. David came away from his first couple of weeks wondering just what or who had held Energix together—and feeling more convinced than ever that he could push this company to the next level.

But then he began to hit roadblocks. The senior management committee (SMC) meetings started out frustrating and got worse. David, who was used highly disciplined meetings with clear agendas and actionable decisions, found the committee members' elliptical discussions and consensus-driven process agonizing. Particularly troubling to him was the lack of open discussion about pressing issues and the sense that decisions were being made through back channels. When David raised a sensitive or provocative issue with the SMC, or pressed others in the room for commitments to act, people would either fall silent or recite a list of reasons why things couldn't be done a certain way.

Two months in, with his patience frayed, David decided to simply focus on what he had been hired to do: revamp the new-product development processes to support the company's growth. So he convened a meeting of the heads of R&D, operations, and finance to discuss how to proceed. At that gathering, David presented a plan for setting up teams that would map out existing processes and conduct a thorough redesign effort. He also outlined the required resource commitments—for instance, assigning strong people from operations and finance to participate in the teams, and hiring external consultants to support the analysis.

Given the conversations he'd had with the CEO during recruiting and the clear mandate he felt he'd been given, David was shocked by the stonewalling he encountered. The attendees listened but wouldn't commit themselves or their people to David's plan. Instead, they urged David to bring his plan before the whole SMC because it affected many parts of the company and had the potential to be disruptive if not managed carefully. (He later learned that two of the participants had gone to the CEO soon after the meeting to register their concerns; David was "a bull in a china shop," according to one. "We have to be careful not to upset some delicate balances as we get out the next-gen turbine," said the other. And both were of the firm opinion that "letting Jones run things might not be the right way to go.") Even more troubling, David experienced a noticeable and worrisome chill in his relationship with the CEO.

Joining a new company is akin to an organ transplant—and you're the new organ. If you're not thoughtful in adapting to the new situation, you could end up being attacked by the organizational immune system and rejected. Witness David's challenges at Energix.

When surveyed, senior HR practitioners overwhelmingly assess the challenge of coming in from the outside as "much harder" than being promoted from within.[1] They attribute the high failure rate of outside hires to several barriers, notably the following:

- Leaders from outside the company are not familiar with informal networks of information and communication.

- Outside hires are not familiar with the corporate culture and therefore have greater difficulty navigating.

- New people are unknown to the organization and therefore do not have the same credibility as someone who is promoted from within.

- A long tradition of hiring from within makes it difficult for some organizations to accept outsiders.

To overcome these barriers and succeed in joining a new company, you should focus on four pillars of effective onboarding: business orientation, stakeholder connection, alignment of expectations, and cultural adaptation.

Business Orientation

Business orientation is the most straightforward part of onboarding. The sooner you understand the business environment in which you're operating, the sooner you can make productive contributions. Getting oriented to the business means learning about the company as a whole and not only your specific parts of the business. As you work to understand the organization, it's worth thinking beyond simply the financials, products, and strategy. Regardless of your position, for example, it's beneficial to learn about the brands and products you will be supporting, whether or not you're directly involved in sales and marketing. Focus, too, on understanding the operating model, planning and performance evaluation systems, and talent management systems, because they often powerfully influence how you can most effectively have an impact.

Stakeholder Connection

It's also essential to develop the right relationship wiring as soon as possible. This means identifying key stakeholders and building productive working relationships. As with David, there is a natural but dangerous tendency for new leaders to focus on building vertical relationships early in their transitions—up to their bosses and down to their teams. Often, insufficient time is devoted to lateral relationship building with peers and key constituencies outside the new leader's immediate organization. Remember: you don't want to be meeting your neighbors for the first time in the middle of the night when your house is burning down.

Expectations Alignment

No matter how well you think you understand what you're expected to do, be sure to check and recheck expectations once you formally join your new organization. Why? Because understandings that are developed before you join—about mandates, support, and resources—may not prove to be fully accurate once you're in the job. It isn't that you've been actively misled; rather, it's because recruiting is like romance, and employment is like marriage. As David learned, newly hired leaders can easily come to believe that they have more latitude to make changes than is actually the case. If they act on these sorts of incorrect assumptions, they easily can trigger unnecessary resistance and even derail themselves.

It also is important to understand and factor in the expectations of key constituencies other than your new boss—for example, key people in finance at corporate headquarters if you're working in a business unit. This is especially the case if they're likely to influence how you're evaluated and rewarded.

Cultural Adaptation

The most daunting challenge for leaders joining new organizations is adapting to unfamiliar cultures. For David, this meant making the transition from an authority-driven, process-focused culture to a consensus-oriented, relational one.

To adapt successfully, you need to understand what the culture is overall and how it's manifested in the organization or unit you're joining (because different units may have different subcultures). In doing this, it helps to think of yourself as an anthropologist sent to study a newly discovered civilization.

What is *culture*? It's a set of consistent patterns people follow for communicating, thinking, and acting, all grounded in their shared assumptions and values. The culture in any organization is generally multilayered, as illustrated in figure 1-2. At the top of the culture pyramid are the surface elements—the symbols, shared languages, and other things most visible to outsiders. Obvious symbols include organizational logos, the way people dress, and the way office space is organized and allocated.

Likewise, every organization typically has a shared language— a long list of acronyms, for instance, describing business units, products, processes, projects, and other elements of the company.

FIGURE 1-2

The culture pyramid

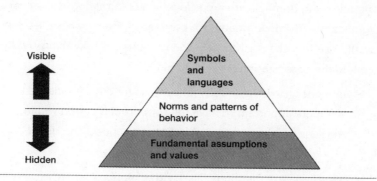

So it's essential that you invest early on in learning to speak like the locals. At this level, it's relatively easy for newcomers to figure out how to fit in. If people at your level don't wear plaid, then you shouldn't either, unless you're trying to signal an intention to change the culture.

Beneath the surface layer of symbols and language lies a deeper, less visible set of organizational norms and accepted patterns of behavior. These elements of culture include things like how people get support for important initiatives, how they win recognition for their accomplishments, and how they view meetings—are they seen as forums for discussion or rubber-stamp sessions? (See the box "Identifying Cultural Norms.") These norms and patterns often are difficult to discern and become evident only after you've spent some time in a new environment.

And finally, underlying all cultures are the fundamental assumptions that everyone has about the way the world works—the shared values that infuse and reinforce all the other elements in the pyramid. A good example is the general beliefs people in the company have about the right way to distribute power

Identifying Cultural Norms

The following domains are areas in which cultural norms may vary significantly from company to company. Transitioning leaders should use this checklist to help them figure out how things really work in the organizations they're joining.

- **Influence.** How do people get support for critical initiatives? Is it more important to have the support of a patron within the senior team, or affirmation from your peers and direct reports that your idea is a good one?

- **Meetings.** Are meetings filled with dialogue on hard issues, or are they simply forums for publicly ratifying agreements that have been reached in private?

- **Execution.** When it comes time to get things done, which matters more—a deep understanding of processes or knowing the right people?

- **Conflict.** Can people talk openly about difficult issues without fear of retribution? Or do they avoid conflict—or, even worse, push it to lower levels, where it can wreak havoc?

- **Recognition.** Does the company promote stars, rewarding those who visibly and vocally drive business initiatives? Or does it encourage team players, rewarding those who lead authoritatively but quietly and collaboratively?

- **Ends versus means.** Are there any restrictions on how you achieve results? Does the organization have a well-defined, well-communicated set of values that is reinforced through positive and negative incentives?

based on position. Are executives in particular roles given lots of decision-making power from Day 1, or is the degree of authority a function of seniority? Or does the organization operate according to consensus, where the ability to persuade is key? Again, these elements of the culture are often invisible and can take time to become clear.

Armed with a deeper understanding of the business situation, political networks, expectations, and culture, you will be in a much stronger position to figure out how to strike the right balance between adapting to the new organization and working to alter it. See table 1-1 for issues and action items related to each of the four pillars as you onboard into a new organization.

The challenges of entering new cultures arise not only when new leaders are transitioning between two different companies, but also when they move between units—the "inboarding" challenge—as well as when they make international moves. Why? It's because both kinds of change typically require new leaders to grapple with new work cultures. The same basic approach to cultural assessment and adaptation can be applied (with suitable modifications) in these situations.[2]

Preparing Yourself

With a deeper understanding of the types of transition challenges you face, you can now focus on preparing yourself to make the leap. How can you be sure to meet the challenges of your new position? You can focus on basic principles for getting ready for your new role, as discussed next.

TABLE 1-1

Onboarding checklists

Business orientation checklist

- As early as possible, get access to publicly available information about financials, products, strategy, and brands.
- Identify additional sources of information, such as websites and analyst reports.
- If appropriate for your level, ask the business to assemble a briefing book.
- If possible, schedule familiarization tours of key facilities before the formal start date.

Stakeholder connection checklist

- Ask your boss to identify and introduce you to the key people you should connect with early on.
- If possible, meet with some stakeholders before the formal start.
- Take control of your calendar, and schedule early meetings with key stakeholders.
- Be careful to focus on lateral relationships (peers, others) and not only vertical ones (boss, direct reports).

Expectations alignment checklist

- Understand and engage in business planning and performance management.
- No matter how well you think you understand what you need to do, schedule a conversation with your boss about expectations in your first week.
- Have explicit conversations about working styles with bosses and direct reports as early as possible.

Cultural adaptation checklist

- During recruiting, ask questions about the organization's culture.
- Schedule conversations with your new boss and HR to discuss work culture, and check back with them regularly.
- Identify people inside the organization who could serve as culture interpreters.
- After thirty days, conduct an informal 360-degree check-in with your boss and peers to gauge how adaptation is proceeding.

Establish a Clear Breakpoint

The move from one position to another usually happens in a blur. You rarely get much notice before being thrust into a new job. If you're lucky, you get a couple of weeks, but more often the move is measured in days. You get caught up in a scramble to finish your old job even as you try to wrap your arms around the new one. Even worse, you may be pressured to perform both jobs until your previous position is filled, making the line of demarcation even fuzzier.

Because you may not get a clean transition in job responsibilities, it is essential to discipline yourself to make the transition mentally. Pick a specific time, such as a weekend, and use it to imagine yourself making the shift. Consciously think of letting go of the old job and embracing the new one. Think hard about the differences between the two, and consider how you must now think and act differently. Take the time to celebrate your move, even informally, with family and friends. Use the time to touch base with your informal advisers and counselors and to ask for advice. The bottom line: do whatever it takes to get into the transition state of mind.

Assess Your Vulnerabilities

You have been offered your new position because those who selected you think you have the skills to succeed. But as you saw in the cases of Julia Gould and David Jones, it can be fatal to rely too much on what made you successful in the past.

One way to pinpoint your vulnerabilities is to assess your *problem preferences*—the kinds of problems toward which you naturally gravitate. Everyone likes to do some things more than others. Julia's preference was marketing; for others, it may be finance or operations. Your preferences have probably influenced you to choose jobs where you can do more of what you like to do. As a result, you've perfected those skills and feel most competent when you solve problems in those areas, and that reinforces the cycle. This pattern is like exercising your right arm and ignoring your left: the strong arm gets stronger, and the weak one atrophies. The risk, of course, is that you create an imbalance that leaves you vulnerable when success depends on being ambidextrous.

Table 1-2 is a simple tool for assessing your preferences for different kinds of business problems. Fill in each cell by assessing your intrinsic interest in *solving problems* in the domain in question. In the upper-left cell, for example, ask yourself how much you like to work on appraisal and reward systems. This isn't a comparative question; don't compare this interest with others.

TABLE 1-2

Assessment of problem preferences

Assess your intrinsic interest in solving problems in each of these domains on a scale of 1 to 10, where 1 means very little interest and 10 means a great deal of interest.

Design of appraisal and reward systems	Employee morale	Equity/fairness
Management of financial risk	Budgeting	Cost-consciousness
Product positioning	Relationships with customers	Organizational customer focus
Product or service quality	Relationships with distributors and suppliers	Continuous improvement
Project management systems	Relationships among R&D, marketing, and operations	Cross-functional cooperation

Rank your interest in each cell separately, on a scale of 1 (not at all) to 10 (very much). Keep in mind that you're being asked about your intrinsic *interests* and not your skills or experience. Do not turn the page before completing the table.

Now transfer your rankings from table 1-2 to the corresponding cells in table 1-3. Then sum the three columns and the five rows.

The column totals represent your preferences among technical, political, and cultural problems. *Technical* problems encompass strategies, markets, technologies, and processes. *Political* problems concern power and politics in the organization. *Cultural* problems involve values, norms, and guiding assumptions.

If one column total is noticeably lower than the others, it represents a potential blind spot for you. If you score high on technical interests and low on cultural or political interests, for example, you may be at risk of overlooking the human side of the organizational equation.

The row totals represent your preferences for the various business functions. A low score in any row suggests that you prefer not to grapple with problems in that functional area. Again, these are potential blind spots.

TABLE 1-3
_____

Preferences for problems and functions

	Technical	Political	Cultural	Total
Human resources				
Finance				
Marketing				
Operations				
Research and development				
Total				

The results of this diagnostic exercise should help you answer the following questions: in what spheres do you most enjoy solving problems? In what spheres are you *least* eager to solve problems? What are the implications for potential vulnerabilities in your new position?

You can do a lot to compensate for your vulnerabilities. Three basic tools are self-discipline, team building, and advice and counsel. You need to discipline yourself to devote time to critical activities that you do not enjoy and that may not come naturally. Beyond that, actively search out people in your organization whose skills are sharp in these areas, so that they can serve as a backstop for you and you can learn from them. A network of advisers and counselors can also help you move beyond your comfort zone.

Watch Out for Your Strengths

Your weaknesses can make you vulnerable, but so can your strengths. To paraphrase Abraham Maslow, "To a person with a hammer, everything looks like a nail."[3] The qualities that have made you successful so far (it's worth being clear in your own mind what your hammer is) can prove to be weaknesses in your new role. For example, Julia was highly attentive to detail. Though clearly a strength, her attention to detail had a downside, especially in tandem with a high need for control: the result was a tendency to micromanage people in the areas she knew best. This behavior demoralized people who wanted to make their own contributions without intrusive oversight.

Relearn How to Learn

It may have been some time since you faced a steep learning curve. "Suddenly I realized how much I didn't know" is a common lament from leaders in transition. You may have excelled in a function or discipline, like Julia, and now find yourself in a project-leadership position. Or like David, you may be joining a new company where you lack an established network and sense of the culture. In any case, you suddenly need to learn a lot, fast.

Having to start learning again can evoke long-buried and unnerving feelings of incompetence or vulnerability, especially if you suffer early setbacks. You may find yourself mentally revisiting a juncture in your career when you had less confidence. Perhaps you will make some early missteps and experience failure for the first time in ages. So you unconsciously begin to gravitate toward areas where you feel competent and toward people who reinforce your feelings of self-worth.

New challenges and associated fears of incompetence can set up a vicious cycle of denial and defensiveness. Put bluntly, you can decide to learn and adapt, or you can become brittle and fail. Your failure may be dramatic, like Julia's, or it may be death by a thousand cuts, but it is inevitable. As I discuss in the next chapter on accelerating your learning, denial and defensiveness are a sure recipe for disaster.

Relearning how to learn can be stressful. So if you find yourself waking up in a cold sweat, take comfort. Most new leaders experience the same feelings. And if you embrace the need to learn, you can surmount them.

Rework Your Network

As you advance in your career, the advice you need changes. Preparing yourself for a new role calls for proactively restructuring your advice-and-counsel network. Early in your career, there is a premium on cultivating good technical advisers—experts in certain aspects of marketing or finance, for instance, who can help you get your work done. As you move to higher levels, however, it becomes increasingly important to get good political counsel and personal advice. Political counselors help you understand the politics of the organization, an understanding that is especially important when you plan to implement change. Personal advisers help you keep perspective and equilibrium in times of stress. Transforming your advice-and-counsel network is never easy; your current advisers may be close friends, and you may feel comfortable with technical advisers whose domains you know well. But it is essential to step back and recognize where you need to build your networks to compensate for blind spots and gaps in your own expertise or experience.

Watch Out for People Who Want to Hold You Back

Consciously or not, some individuals may not want you to advance. Your old boss, for example, may not want to let you go. So you must negotiate clear expectations, as soon as you know when you will be transitioning, about what you will do to close things out. This means being specific about the issues or projects that will be dealt with and to what extent—and, critically, what is *not* going to be done. Take notes, and circulate them back to the boss so that everyone is on the same page. Then hold your boss, and yourself, to the agreement. Be realistic about what you can accomplish. There is always more you could do, so keep in mind that time to learn and plan before you enter a new job is a precious commodity.

Colleagues who have become subordinates may not want their relationships with you to change; this challenge is especially sharp when you're promoted to lead former peers. But change they must, and the sooner you accept that (and help others accept it, too), the better. Others in your organization will be looking for signs of favoritism and will judge you accordingly.

If you have been promoted to supervise people who were once your peers, some may be disappointed competitors. Some may even work to undermine you. This kind of thing may subside with time. But expect early tests of your authority, and plan to meet them by being firm and fair. If you don't establish limits early, you will live to regret it. Getting others to accept your move is an essential part of preparing yourself. So if you conclude that the people in question are never going to accept your new role and the resulting situation, then you must find a way to move them out of your organization as quickly as possible.

Get Some Help

Many organizations have programs and processes to help leaders make successful transitions. These range from high-potential development programs (which prepare promising leaders for senior levels) to formal onboarding processes (programs or coaching) that focus on key imperatives. You should take advantage of all the organization has to offer.

However, even if your new organization doesn't have formal transition support, you should engage with HR and your new boss about creating a 90-day transition plan. If you have been promoted, find out whether there are competency models describing the requirements of your new role (but don't assume they tell the whole story). If you have been hired from the outside, ask for help in identifying and connecting with key stakeholders or finding a cultural interpreter. These people often are natural historians who can give you insight into how the organization has evolved and changed.

Closing the Loop

Preparing yourself for a new role turns out to be hard work, and some of the barriers may lie within you. Take a few minutes to think hard about your personal vulnerabilities in your new role, as revealed by your analysis of your problem preferences. How will you compensate for them? Then think about the external forces, such as commitments to your current boss, that could hold you back. How can you avoid that outcome?

To borrow an old saw, preparing yourself is a journey and not a destination. You will have to work constantly to ensure that you're engaging with the real challenges of your new position and not retreating to your comfort zone. It is easy to backslide into habits that are both comfortable and dangerous. Plan to reread this chapter and its questions periodically, asking, Am I doing all I can to prepare myself?

PREPARE YOURSELF—CHECKLIST

1. If you have been promoted, what are the implications for your need to balance breadth and depth, delegate, influence, communicate, and exhibit leadership presence?

2. If you are joining a new organization, how will you orient yourself to the business, identify and connect with key stakeholders, clarify expectations, and adapt to the new culture? What is the right balance between adapting to the new situation and trying to alter it?

3. What has made you successful so far in your career? Can you succeed in your new position by relying solely on those strengths? If not, what are the critical skills you need to develop?

4. Are there aspects of your new job that are critical to success but that you prefer not to focus on? Why? How will you compensate for your potential blind spots?

5. How can you ensure that you make the mental leap into the new position? From whom might you seek advice and counsel on this? What other activities might help you do this?

CHAPTER 2

Accelerate Your Learning

Chris Hadley headed the quality assurance function at Dura Corporation, a medium-sized software services company. When Chris's boss left to become vice president of operations at Phoenix Systems, a struggling software developer, he asked Chris to join him as head of the product quality and testing unit. Although it was a lateral move, Chris jumped at the opportunity to lead a turnaround.

Dura was a world-class software development operation. Chris had joined the company right out of engineering school and had risen rapidly in the quality function. He was highly skilled; however, he had grown up in an environment with state-of-the-art technology and a motivated workforce. Having visited the Phoenix product testing group before taking the job, Chris knew that it did not come close to measuring up. He was determined to change that—and quickly.

Soon after arriving, Chris declared Phoenix's existing processes outdated and went on record as saying that the operation needed to be rebuilt from the ground up "the Dura way." He immediately brought in operations consultants, who delivered a scathing report, characterizing the Phoenix's testing technology and systems as "antiquated" and the skills of the workforce as "inadequate." They recommended a thorough reorganization of the product testing process as well as substantial investments in technology and worker training. Chris shared this information with his direct reports, saying that he planned to act quickly on the recommendations, starting with a reorganization of the product testing teams "the way we did things at Dura."

Only a month after the new structure was put in place, productivity in the unit plummeted, threatening to delay the launch of a key new product. Chris convened his direct reports and urged them to "get the problems fixed, and fast." But the problems remained, and morale throughout the operation slumped.

After only two months in his new role, Chris's boss told him, "You've alienated just about everyone. I brought you here to improve quality, not tear it down." His boss then peppered him with questions: "How much time did you spend learning about the operation? Did you know they've been asking for more investment for years? Have you seen what they were able to accomplish before you arrived with the resources they were given? You've got to stop doing and start listening."

Shaken, Chris held sobering discussions with his managers, supervisors, and groups of workers. He learned a lot about the creativity they had displayed in dealing with the lack of investment in the operation. He also got direct feedback about what was not working with his new structure. He called an all-hands meeting and announced that, based on the feedback he had received, there would be significant adjustments to the structure.

He also committed to upgrading testing technology and training before making any other changes.

What did Chris do wrong? Like many new leaders, he failed to focus on learning about his new organization and so made some bad decisions that undercut his credibility.

The first task in making a successful transition is to accelerate your learning. Effective learning gives you the foundational insights you need as you build your plan for the next 90 days. So it is essential to figure out what you need to know about your new organization and then to learn it as rapidly as you can. The more efficiently and effectively you learn, the more quickly you will close your window of vulnerability. You can identify potential problems that might erupt and take you offtrack. The faster you climb the learning curve, the earlier you can begin to make good business decisions.

Overcoming Learning Roadblocks

When a new leader derails, failure to learn effectively is almost always a factor. Early in your transition you inevitably feel as if you are drinking from a fire hose. There is so much to absorb that it's difficult to know where to focus. Amid the torrent of information coming your way, it's easy to miss important signals. Or you might focus too much on the technical side of the business—products, customers, technologies, and strategies—and shortchange critical learning about culture and politics.

To compound this problem, surprisingly few managers have received training in systematically diagnosing organizations. Those who have had such training invariably prove to be either human resource professionals or former management consultants.

A related problem is a failure to plan to learn. *Planning to learn* means figuring out in advance what the important questions are and how you can best answer them. Few new leaders take the time to think systematically about their learning priorities. Fewer still explicitly create a learning plan when entering a new role.

Some leaders even have "learning roadblocks," internal barriers to learning. One example is Chris's failure to focus on understanding the history of the organization. A baseline question you always should ask is, "How did we get to this point?" Otherwise, you risk tearing down existing structures or processes without knowing why they were put there in the first place. Armed with insight into the organization's history, you may indeed decide that things need to change. Or you may find there is a good reason to leave it exactly where it is.

A related learning block, as mentioned in the introduction, is the action imperative. The primary symptom is a nearly compulsive need to take action. Effective leaders strike the right balance between doing (making things happen) and being (observing and reflecting). But it is challenging, as Chris Hadley found, to let yourself "be" during transitions. And the pressure to "do" almost always comes more from inside the leader than from outside forces; it reflects a lack of confidence and a consequent need to prove yourself. Remember: simply displaying a genuine desire to learn and understand translates into increased credibility and influence.

So if you habitually find yourself too anxious or too busy to devote time to learning, you may suffer from the action imperative. It is a serious affliction, because often, being too busy to learn results in a death spiral. If, like Chris, you do not focus on learning, you can easily make poor early decisions that undermine your credibility, alienate potential supporters, and make people less likely to share important information with you. The result is that you make more bad decisions and enter a vicious cycle that can irreparably damage your credibility. So beware. It may feel right to enter a new situation and begin acting decisively—and sometimes, as you will see in the next chapter, it *is* the right thing to do—but you risk being poorly prepared to see the real problems.

Perhaps most destructive of all, some new leaders arrive, as Chris did at Phoenix, with "the" answer. They have already made up their minds about what the organization's problems are and how to solve them. Having matured in organizations where things were done "the right way," these leaders fail to realize that what works well in one organization may fail miserably in another. As Chris found out the hard way, coming in with the answer leaves you vulnerable to making serious mistakes and is likely to alienate people. Chris thought he could simply import what he had learned at Dura to fix the Phoenix plant's problems.

Leaders who are onboarding into new organizations must therefore focus on learning and adapting to the new culture. Otherwise they risk suffering the organizational equivalent of organ rejection syndrome (with the new leaders being the organs). They do things that trigger the organization's immune system and find themselves under attack as a foreign body. Even in situations (such as turnarounds) when you have been brought in explicitly to import new ways of doing things, you still have to learn about the organization's culture and politics to socialize and customize your approach.

Managing Learning as an Investment Process

If you approach your efforts to get up to speed as an investment process—and your scarce time and energy as resources that deserve careful management—you will realize returns in the form of actionable insights. An *actionable insight* is knowledge that enables you to make better decisions earlier and so helps you quickly reach the break-even point in personal value creation. Chris would have acted differently if he had known that (1) senior management at Phoenix had systematically underinvested in the past, despite energetic efforts by local managers to upgrade, (2) the operation had achieved remarkable results in quality and productivity given what it had to work with, and (3) the supervisors and workforce were justifiably proud of what they had accomplished.

To maximize your return on investment in learning, you must effectively and efficiently extract actionable insights from the mass of information available to you. Effective learning calls for figuring out *what* you need to learn so that you can focus your efforts. Devote some time to defining your learning agenda as early as possible, and return to it periodically to refine and supplement it. Efficient learning means identifying the best available sources of insight and then figuring out how to extract maximum insight with the least possible outlay of time. Chris's approach to learning about the Phoenix operation was neither effective nor efficient.

Defining Your Learning Agenda

If Chris had it to do over, what might he have done? He would have planned to engage in a systematic learning process—creating a virtuous cycle of information gathering, analyzing, hypothesizing, and testing.

The starting point is to begin to define your learning agenda, ideally before you formally enter the organization. A learning agenda crystallizes your learning priorities: what do you most need to learn? It consists of a focused set of questions to guide your inquiry or the hypotheses you want to explore and test, or both. Of course, learning during a transition is iterative: at first, your learning agenda will consist mostly of questions, but as you learn more, you will hypothesize about what is going on and why. Increasingly, your learning will shift toward fleshing out and testing those hypotheses.

How should you compile your early list of guiding questions? Start by generating questions about the past, the present, and the future (see boxes, "Questions About the Past," "Questions About the Present," and "Questions About the Future"). Why are things done the way they are? Are the reasons something was done (for example, to meet a competitive threat) still valid? Are conditions changing so that something different should be done in the future? The accompanying boxes offer sample questions in these three categories.

Questions About the Past

Performance

- How has this organization performed in the past? How do people in the organization think it has performed?

- How were goals set? Were they insufficiently or overly ambitious?

- Were internal or external benchmarks used?

- What measures were employed? What behaviors did they encourage and discourage?

- What happened if goals were not met?

Root Causes

- If performance has been good, why has that been the case?

- What have been the relative contributions of strategy, structure, systems, talent bases, culture, and politics?

- If performance has been poor, why has that been the case? Do the primary issues reside in the organization's strategy? Its structure? Its technical capabilities? Its culture? Its politics?

History of Change

- What efforts have been made to change the organization? What happened?

- Who has been instrumental in shaping this organization?

Questions About the Present

Vision and Strategy

- What is the stated vision and strategy?

- Is the organization really pursuing that strategy? If not, why not? If so, will the strategy take the organization where it needs to go?

People

- Who is capable, and who is not?

- Who is trustworthy, and who is not?

- Who has influence, and why?

Processes

- What are the key processes?

- Are they performing acceptably in quality, reliability, and timeliness? If not, why not?

Land Mines

- What lurking surprises could detonate and push you offtrack?

- What potentially damaging cultural or political missteps must you avoid?

Early Wins

- In what areas (people, relationships, processes, or products) can you achieve some early wins?

Questions About the Future

Challenges and Opportunities

- In what areas is the organization most likely to face stiff challenges in the coming year? What can be done now to prepare for them?

- What are the most promising unexploited opportunities? What would need to happen to realize their potential?

Barriers and Resources

- What are the most formidable barriers to making needed changes? Are they technical? Cultural? Political?

- Are there islands of excellence or other high-quality resources that you can leverage?

- What new capabilities need to be developed or acquired?

Culture

- Which elements of the culture should be preserved?

- Which elements need to change?

As you work to answer these questions, think, too, about the right mix of technical, interpersonal, cultural, and political learning.[1] In the technical domain, you may have to grapple with unfamiliar markets, technologies, processes, and systems. In the interpersonal domain, you need to get to know your boss, peers, and direct reports. In the cultural domain, you must learn about norms, values, and behavioral expectations, which are almost certainly different from those in the organization you came from, even if you're moving between units in the same company. In the political domain, you must understand the *shadow organization*—the informal set of processes and alliances that exist in the shadow of the formal structure and strongly influence how work actually gets done. The political domain is both important and difficult to understand, because it isn't easily visible to those who have not spent time in the organization and because political land mines can easily stymie your efforts to establish a solid base of support during the transition.

Identifying the Best Sources of Insight

You will learn from various types of hard data, such as financial and operating reports, strategic and functional plans, employee surveys, press accounts, and industry reports. But to make effective decisions, you also need "soft" information about the organization's strategy, technical capabilities, culture, and politics. The only way to gain this intelligence is to talk to people who have critical knowledge about your situation.

Who can provide the best return on your learning investment? Identifying promising sources will make your learning both comprehensive and efficient. Keep in mind that you need to listen to key people both inside and outside the organization (see figure 2-1). Talking to people with different points of view will deepen your insight. Specifically, it will help you translate between external

FIGURE 2-1

Sources of knowledge

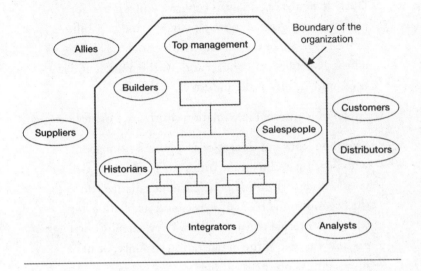

realities and internal perceptions, and between people at the top of the hierarchy and people on the front lines.

The most valuable external sources of information are likely to be the following:

- **Customers.** How do customers—external or internal—perceive your organization? How do your best customers assess your products or services? How about your customer service? If your customers are external, how do they rank your company against your competitors?

- **Suppliers.** Suppliers can give you their perspectives on your organization in its role as a customer. You can also learn about the strengths and flaws of your internal systems for managing quality and customer satisfaction.

- **Distributors.** From distributors, you can learn about the logistics of product movement, customer service, and

competitors' practices and offerings. You can also get a
sense of the distributors' own capabilities.

- **Outside analysts.** Analysts can give you a fairly objective
  assessment of your company's strategy and capabilities
  as well as those of your competitors. Analysts also have
  a broad overview of the demands of the market and the
  economic health of the industry.

Indispensable internal information sources are the following:

- **Frontline R&D and operations.** These are the people
  who develop and manufacture your products or deliver
  your services. Frontline people can familiarize you with
  the organization's basic processes and its relationships
  with key external constituencies. They can also shed light
  on how the rest of the organization supports or under-
  mines efforts on the front line.

- **Sales and procurement.** These people, along with
  customer service representatives and purchasing staff,
  interact directly with customers, distributors, and
  suppliers. Often they have up-to-date information about
  trends and imminent changes in the market.

- **Staff.** Talk with heads or key staff members of the
  finance, legal, and human resource functional areas.
  These people have specialized but useful perspectives on
  the internal workings of the organization.

- **Integrators.** Integrators are people who coordinate or
  facilitate cross-functional interaction, including project
  managers, plant managers, and product managers. You
  can learn from them how links within the company
  work and how the functions mesh. These people also

can help you discover the true political hierarchies and identify where internal conflicts lie.

- **Natural historians.** Keep an eye out for "old-timers" or natural historians—people who have been with the organization for a long time and who naturally absorb its history. From these people, you can learn about the company's mythology (key stories about how the organization came to be and trials it has gone through) and the roots of its culture and politics.

If you are new to the organization, there often is much you can do to accelerate the onboarding process before you arrive. The starting point, beyond the recruiting process, is to leverage the rich array of resources available online, including background information and analysis of the organization, biographies of key people, and information available on the organization's own website. Beyond that, it is highly desirable, if possible, to reach out to current or former employees to get a bead on the history and culture.

Adopting Structured Learning Methods

Once you have a rough sense of what you need to learn and where to seek it—whether from reports, conversations with knowledgeable people, or electronic resources—the next step is to understand how best to learn.

Many leaders tend to dive in and start talking to people. You will pick up much soft information in this way, but it is not efficient. That's because it can be time-consuming and because its lack of structure makes it difficult to know how much weight to place on various individuals' observations. Your views may be shaped excessively by the first few people (or last few) with whom you talk. And people may seek you out early precisely to influence you.

Instead, you should consider using a structured learning process. To illustrate the advantages of this approach, imagine that you plan to meet with your direct reports to elicit their assessments. How might you go about doing this? Bringing them together right away might be a mistake, because some people will hesitate to reveal their views in a public forum.

So you might start by meeting them one-on-one. Of course, this method has its drawbacks, too, because you have to meet people in some order. You should therefore expect that the people who are later on your schedule will talk to the earlier ones to try to get a sense of what you're after. This may reduce your ability to gain a range of views and may allow others to interpret your messages in ways you might not intend.

Suppose you decide to meet with your direct reports one-on-one. In what order will you meet with them? And how will you avoid being excessively influenced by what the first couple of people say? One approach is to keep to the same script in all your meetings. You might start with brief opening remarks about yourself and your approach, followed by questions about the other person (background, family, and interests) and then a standard set of questions about the business. This approach is powerful, because the responses you get are comparable. You can line them up side by side and analyze what is consistent and inconsistent about the responses. This comparison helps you gain insight into which people are being more or less open.

When you are diagnosing a new organization, start by meeting with your direct reports one-on-one. (This is an example of taking a horizontal slice across an organization by interviewing people at the same level in different functions.) Ask them essentially the same five questions:

1. What are the biggest challenges the organization is facing (or will face in the near future)?

2. Why is the organization facing (or going to face) these challenges?

3. What are the most promising unexploited opportunities for growth?

4. What would need to happen for the organization to exploit the potential of these opportunities?

5. If you were me, what would you focus attention on?

These five questions, coupled with careful listening and thoughtful follow-up, are certain to elicit many insights; think of what Chris might have learned by using this approach. By asking everyone the same set of questions, you can identify prevalent and divergent views and thus avoid being swayed by the first or most forceful or articulate person you talk to. How people answer can also tell you a lot about your new team and its politics. Who answers directly, and who is evasive or prone to tangents? Who takes responsibility, and who points fingers? Who has a broad view of the business, and who seems stuck in a silo?

Once you have distilled these early discussions into a set of observations, questions, and insights, convene your direct reports as a group, feed them back your impressions and questions, and invite discussion. You will learn about both substance and team dynamics and will simultaneously demonstrate how quickly you have begun to identify key issues.

You need not follow this process rigidly. You could, for example, get an outside consultant to do some diagnosis of the organization and feed back the results to your group (see "Assimilating New Leaders"). Or you could invite an internal facilitator to run the process. The point is that even a modest structure—a script and a sequence of interactions, such as meeting with people individually, doing some analysis, and then meeting with them together—can dramatically accelerate your ability to extract actionable insights. Naturally, the questions you ask will be tailored for the groups you meet. If you're meeting with salespeople, for example, consider asking, What do our customers want that they're getting from our competitors and not getting from us?

Assimilating New Leaders

One example of a structured learning method is the new leader assimilation process originally developed by GE. In this process, each time a manager enters a significant new role, he is assigned a transition facilitator. The facilitator meets first with the new leader to lay out the process. This is followed by a meeting with the leader's new direct reports in which they are asked questions such as, What would you like to know about the new leader? What would you like him to know about you? About the business situation? The main findings are then fed back, without attribution, to the new leader. The process ends with a facilitated meeting between the new leader and the direct reports.

Another example of a structured learning method is the use of a framework such as SWOT (strengths, weaknesses, opportunities, and threats) analysis to guide your diagnostic work. These sorts of frameworks also can be powerful tools for communicating with key stakeholders—bosses, peers, and direct reports—to help create shared views of the situation. Other structured learning methods are valuable in particular situations. Some of the methods described in table 2-1 may increase the efficiency of your learning process depending on your level in the organization and the business situation. Effective new leaders employ a

TABLE 2-1

Structured methods for learning

Method	Uses	Useful for
Organizational climate and employee satisfaction surveys	Learning about culture and morale. Many organizations do such surveys regularly, and a database may already be available. If not, consider setting up a regular survey of employee perceptions.	Useful for managers at all levels if the analysis is available specifically for your unit or group. Usefulness depends on the granularity of the collection and analysis. This also assumes the survey instrument is a good one and the data has been collected carefully and analyzed rigorously.
Structured sets of interviews with slices of the organization or unit	Identifying shared and divergent perceptions of opportunities and problems. You can interview people at the same level in different departments (a horizontal slice) or bore down through multiple levels (a vertical slice). Whichever dimension you choose, ask everybody the same questions, and look for similarities and differences in people's responses.	Most useful for managers leading groups of people from different functional backgrounds. Can be useful at lower levels if the unit is experiencing significant problems.
Focus groups	Probing issues that preoccupy key groups of employees, such as morale issues among frontline production or service workers. Gathering groups of people who work together also lets you see how they interact and identify who displays leadership. Fostering discussion promotes deeper insight.	Most useful for managers of large groups of people who perform a similar function, such as sales managers or plant managers. Can be useful for senior managers as a way of getting quick insights into the perceptions of key employee constituencies.

(Continued)

TABLE 2-1

Structured methods for learning *(continued)*

Method	Uses	Useful for
Analysis of critical past decisions	Illuminating decision-making patterns and sources of power and influence. Select an important recent decision, and look into how it was made. Who exerted influence at each stage? Talk with the people involved, probe their perceptions, and note what is and is not said.	Most useful for higher-level managers of business units or project groups.
Process analysis	Examining interactions among departments or functions and assessing the efficiency of a process. Select an important process, such as delivery of products to customers or distributors, and assign a cross-functional group to chart the process and identify bottlenecks and problems.	Most useful for managers of units or groups in which the work of multiple functional specialties must be integrated. Can be useful for lower-level managers as a way of understanding how their groups fit into larger processes.
Plant and market tours	Learning firsthand from people close to the product. Plant tours let you meet production personnel informally and listen to their concerns. Meetings with sales and production staff help you assess technical capabilities. Market tours can introduce you to customers, whose comments can reveal problems and opportunities.	Most useful for managers of business units.
Pilot projects	Gaining deep insight into technical capabilities, culture, and politics. Although these insights are not the primary purpose of pilot projects, you can learn a lot from how the organization or group responds to your pilot initiatives.	Useful for managers at all levels. The size of the pilot projects and their impact will increase as you rise through the organization.

combination of methods, tailoring their learning strategy to the demands of the situation.

Creating a Learning Plan

Your *learning agenda* defines what you want to learn. Your *learning plan* defines how you will go about learning it. It translates learning goals into specific sets of actions—identifying promising sources of insight and using systematic methods—that accelerate your learning. Your learning plan is a critical part of your overall 90-day plan. In fact, as you will discover later, learning should be a primary focus of your plan for your first 30 days on the job (unless, of course, there is a disaster in progress).

The heart of your learning plan is a cyclical learning process in which you collect information, analyze and distill it, and develop and test hypotheses, thus progressively deepening your understanding of your new organization. Obviously, the specific insights you decide to pursue will vary from situation to situation. You can begin by working with the learning plan template shown here (see box, "Learning Plan Template"). In chapter 3, you will explore various types of transition situations and return to the subject of what you need to learn and when.

Learning Plan Template

Before Entry

- Find out whatever you can about the organization's strategy, structure, performance, and people.

- Look for external assessments of the performance of the organization. You will learn how knowledgeable, fairly

---

unbiased people view it. If you are a manager at a lower level, talk to people who deal with your new group as suppliers or customers.

- Find external observers who know the organization well, including former employees, recent retirees, and people who have transacted business with the organization. Ask these people open-ended questions about history, politics, and culture. Talk with your predecessor if possible.

- Talk to your new boss.

- As you begin to learn about the organization, write down your first impressions and eventually some hypotheses.

- Compile an initial set of questions to guide your structured inquiry after you arrive.

Soon After Entry

- Review detailed operating plans, performance data, and personnel data.

- Meet one-on-one with your direct reports and ask them the questions you compiled. You will learn about convergent and divergent views and about your reports as people.

- Assess how things are going at key interfaces. You will hear how salespeople, purchasing agents, customer service representatives, and others perceive your organization's dealings with external constituencies. You will also learn about problems they see that others do not.

- Test strategic alignment from the top down. Ask people at the top what the company's vision and strategy are. Then see how far down into the organizational hierarchy those beliefs penetrate. You will learn how well the previous leader drove vision and strategy down through the organization.

- Test awareness of challenges and opportunities from the bottom up. Start by asking frontline people how they view the company's challenges and opportunities. Then work your way up. You will learn how well the people at the top check the pulse of the organization.

- Update your questions and hypotheses.

- Meet with your boss to discuss your hypotheses and findings.

By the End of the First Month

- Gather your team to feed back to them your preliminary findings. You will elicit confirmation and challenges of your assessments and will learn more about the group and its dynamics.

- Now analyze key interfaces from the outside in. You will learn how people on the outside (suppliers, customers, distributors, and others) perceive your organization and its strengths and weaknesses.

- Analyze a couple of key processes. Convene representatives of the responsible groups to map out and evaluate the processes you selected. You will learn about productivity, quality, and reliability.

- Meet with key integrators. You will learn how things work at interfaces among functional areas. What problems do they perceive that others do not? Seek out the natural historians. They can fill you in on the history, culture, and politics of the organization, and they are also potential allies and influencers.

- Update your questions and hypotheses.

- Meet with your boss again to discuss your observations.

Getting Help

The primary responsibility for accelerating your learning rests on you, the leader. However, there are many other players whose support can make the learning process a lot less painful. There is much that bosses, peers, and even direct reports can do to accelerate your learning. However, to enlist their aid you need to be clear about what you're trying to do and how they can help. Critically, you need to be willing to ask in the first place and not feel that you should know everything and be in complete control from the moment you walk through the door.

Support for learning is particularly important for leaders joining new organizations. This is true whether you have been hired from the outside (onboarding) or making a move between units in the same organization (inboarding, which, as discussed earlier, is roughly 70 percent as difficult as being hired from the outside). In both cases, you likely will enter a different culture and will lack the political wiring you had in your previous role. If your new organization has an effective onboarding system, it should help you understand the culture and speed the process of identifying and connecting with key stakeholders. If it doesn't, ask for this type of help.

Closing the Loop

Your learning priorities and strategies will inevitably shift as you dig deeper. As you start to interact with your new boss, figure out where to get some early wins, or build supportive coalitions, it will be critical for you to gain additional insights. So plan to return to this chapter periodically to reassess your learning agenda and create new learning plans.

ACCELERATE YOUR LEARNING—CHECKLIST

1. How effective are you at learning about new organizations? Do you sometimes fall prey to the action imperative? To coming in with "the" answer? If so, how will you avoid doing this?

2. What is your learning agenda? Based on what you know now, compose a list of questions to guide your early inquiries. If you have begun to form hypotheses about what is going on, what are they, and how will you test them?

3. Given the questions you want to answer, who is likely to provide you with the most useful insights?

4. How might you increase the efficiency of your learning process? What are some structured ways you might extract more insight for your investment of time and energy?

5. What support is available to accelerate your learning, and how might you best leverage it?

6. Given your answers to the previous questions, start to create your learning plan.

CHAPTER 3

Match Strategy to Situation

If Karl Lewin knew anything, it was how to manage in times of crisis. In fact, he'd recently overseen a quick and successful turnaround of European manufacturing operations at Global Foods, a multinational consumer products company. He was less sure, however, that the same sort of approach would be effective in his new role at the firm.

A hard-driving, German-born executive, Karl had acted decisively in Europe to restructure an organization that was broken because of the company's overemphasis on growth through acquisition and its focus on country-level operations to the exclusion of other opportunities. Within a year, Karl had centralized the most important manufacturing support functions, closed four of the least efficient plants, and shifted a big chunk of production to Eastern Europe. These changes, painful though they were, began to bear fruit by the end of eighteen months, and operational efficiency improved dramatically.

But no good deed goes unpunished. Karl's success in Europe led to his appointment as the executive vice president of supply chain for the company's core North American operations, headquartered in New Jersey. The job was much bigger than the earlier one, combining manufacturing with strategic sourcing, outbound logistics, and customer service.

In contrast to the situation in Europe, North American operations were not in immediate crisis—something Karl recognized was the essence of the problem. The organization's long-term success had only recently shown signs of slipping. The preceding year, industry benchmarks had placed the company's manufacturing performance slightly below average in overall efficiency, and in the lower one-third in the crucial area of customer satisfaction with on-time delivery. Mediocre scores, to be sure, but nothing that screamed "turnaround."

Meanwhile, Karl's own assessment indicated that serious problems were brewing. The business was addicted to fighting fires; managers reveled in their ability to react well in crises rather than prevent problems in the first place. Karl believed it was only a matter of time before major failures occurred. Furthermore, executives relied too much on gut feelings to make critical decisions, and information systems provided too little of the right kind of objective data. These shortcomings contributed, in Karl's view, to widespread, unfounded optimism about the organization's future.

To take charge successfully, you must have a clear understanding of the situation you are facing and the implications for what you need to do and how you need to do it. From the outset, leaders like Karl need to focus on answering two fundamental questions. The first question is, What kind of change am I being called upon to lead? Only by answering this question will you know how to match your strategy to the situation. The second question is, What kind of change leader am I? Here the answer has implications for how you should adjust your leadership style. Careful diagnosis of the business situation will clarify the challenges, opportunities, and resources available to you.

Using the STARS Model

STARS is an acronym for five common business situations leaders may find themselves moving into: start-up, turnaround, accelerated growth, realignment, and sustaining success. The STARS model outlines the characteristics and challenges of, respectively, launching a venture; getting one back on track; dealing with rapid expansion; reenergizing a once-leading business that's now facing serious problems; and inheriting an organization that is performing well and then taking it to the next level.

In all five of the STARS situations, the eventual goal is the same: a successful and growing business. However, the challenges and opportunities, summarized in table 3-1, vary in predictable ways depending on which situation you are experiencing.

What are the defining features of the five STARS situations? In a *start-up*, you are charged with assembling the capabilities (people, funding, and technology) to get a new business, product, project, or relationship off the ground. This means you can shape the organization from the outset by recruiting your team, playing a major role in defining the agenda, and building the architecture of the business. Participants in a start-up are likely to be more excited and hopeful than members of a troubled group facing failure. But at the same time, employees of a start-up are typically much less focused on key issues than those in a turnaround, simply because the vision, strategy, structures, and systems that channel organizational energy are not yet in place.

TABLE 3-1

The STARS model

	Start-Up	Turnaround	Accelerated growth	Realignment	Sustaining success
	Assembling the capabilities (people, financing, and technology) to get a new business or initiative off the ground	Saving a business or initiative widely acknowledged to be in serious trouble	Managing a rapidly expanding business	Reenergizing a previously successful organization that now faces problems	Preserving the vitality of a successful organization and taking it to the next level
Challenges	Building the strategy, structures, and systems from scratch without a clear framework or boundaries	Reenergizing demoralized employees and other stakeholders	Putting in place structures and systems to permit scaling	Convincing employees that change is necessary	Living in the shadow of the former leader and managing the team he or she created
	Recruiting and welding together a high-performing team	Making effective decisions under time pressure	Integrating many new employees	Carefully restructuring the top team and refocusing the organization	Playing good defense before embarking on too many new initiatives
	Making do with limited resources	Going deep enough with painful cuts and difficult personnel choices			Finding ways to take the business to the next level
Opportunities	You can do things right from the beginning.	Everyone recognizes that change is necessary.	The potential for growth helps to motivate people.	The organization has significant pockets of strength.	A strong team may already be in place.
	People are energized by the possibilities.	Affected constituencies offer significant external support.	People will be inclined to stretch themselves and those who work for them.	People want to continue to see themselves as successful.	People are motivated to continue their history of success.
	There are no rigid preconceptions.	A little success goes a long way.			A foundation for continued success (such as a long product pipeline) may be in place.

In a *turnaround*, you take on a unit or group that is recognized to be in deep trouble and work to get it back on track. A turnaround is the classic burning platform, demanding rapid, decisive action. Most people understand that substantial change is necessary, although they may be in disarray and in significant disagreement about what needs to be done. Turnarounds are ready-fire-aim situations: you need to make the tough calls with less than full knowledge and then adjust as you learn more. In contrast, *realignments* (and *sustaining-success assignments*) are more ready-aim-fire situations. Turning around a failing business requires the new leader to cut it down to a defensible core fast and then begin to build it back up. This painful process, if successful, leaves the business in a sustaining-success situation. If efforts to turn around the business fail, the result often is shutdown or divestiture.

In an *accelerated-growth situation*, the organization has begun to hit its stride, and the hard work of scaling up has begun. This typically means you're putting in the structures, processes, and systems necessary to rapidly expand the business (or project, product, or relationship). You also likely need to hire and onboard a lot of people while making sure they become part of the culture that has made the organization successful thus far. The risks, of course, lie in expanding too much too fast.

Start-ups, turnarounds, and accelerated-growth situations involve much resource-intensive construction work; there isn't much existing infrastructure and capacity for you to build on. To a significant degree, you get to start fresh or, in the case of accelerated growth, to build on a strong foundation. In realignments and sustaining-success situations, in contrast, you enter organizations that have significant strengths but also serious constraints on what you can and cannot do. Fortunately, in these two situations you typically have some time before you need to make major calls. This is good, because you must learn a lot about the culture and politics and begin building supportive coalitions.

Because of internal complacency, erosion of key capabilities, or external challenges, successful businesses tend to drift toward trouble. In a realignment, your challenge is to revitalize a unit, product, process, or project that has been drifting into danger. The clouds are gathering on the horizon, but the storm has not yet broken—and many people may not even see the clouds. The biggest challenge often is to create a sense of urgency. There may be a lot of denial; the leader needs to open people's eyes to the fact that a problem actually exists. This was the situation facing Karl in North America. Here, the good news is that the organization likely has at least islands of significant strength (good products, customer relationships, processes, and people).

In a sustaining-success situation, you are shouldering responsibility for preserving the vitality of a successful organization and taking it to the next level. This emphatically does not mean that the organization can rest on its laurels. Rather, it means you need to understand, at a deep level, what has made the business successful and position it to meet the inevitable challenges so that it will continue to grow and prosper. In fact, the key to sustaining success often lies in continuously starting up, accelerating, and realigning parts of the business.

A key implication is that success in transitioning depends, in no small measure, on your ability to transform the prevailing organizational psychology in predictable ways. In start-ups, the prevailing mood is often one of excited confusion, and your job is to channel that energy into productive directions, in part by deciding what not to do. In turnarounds, you may be dealing with a group of people who are close to despair; it is your job to provide them with a concrete plan for moving forward and confidence that it will improve the situation. In accelerated-growth situations, you need to help people understand that the organization needs to be more disciplined and get them to work within defined processes and systems. In realignments, you will likely have to pierce the veil of denial that is preventing people from confronting the need to reinvent the business. Finally, in sustaining-success situations, you must invent the challenge by finding ways to keep people motivated, combat complacency, and find new direction for growth—both organizational and personal.

You cannot figure out where to take a new organization if you do not understand where it has been and how it got where it is. In Karl's realignment situation, for example, it is essential that he understand what made the organization successful in the past and why it drifted into trouble. To understand your situation, you must put on your historian's hat.

But if you're not leading a large business, can you still use the STARS model to understand the challenges you face? Absolutely. You can apply it regardless of your level in the organization. You may be a new CEO taking over an entire company that is in start-up mode. Or you could be a first-line supervisor managing a new production line, a brand manager launching a new product, an R&D team leader responsible for a new product development project, or an information technology manager responsible for implementing a new enterprise software system. All of these situations share the characteristics of a start-up. Similarly, turnaround, accelerated growth, realignment, and sustaining success arise at all levels, in companies large and small.

Diagnosing Your STARS Portfolio

In reality, you're unlikely to encounter a pure and tidy example of a start-up, turnaround, accelerated-growth, realignment, or sustaining-success situation. At a high level your situation may fit reasonably neatly into one of these categories. But as soon as you drill down, you will almost certainly discover that you're managing a portfolio—of products, projects, processes, plants, or people—that represents a mix of STARS situations. For instance, you may be taking over an organization that enjoys incremental growth with successful products and in which one group is launching a line of products based on a new technology. Or you may be working to turn around a company that has a couple of high-performing, state-of-the-art plants.

The next step in applying the STARS model is to diagnose your STARS portfolio; you must figure out which parts of your new organization belong in each of the five categories. Take time to assign the pieces of your new responsibilities (such as products, processes, projects, plants, and people) to the five categories using table 3-2. Given this arrangement, how will you manage the various pieces differently? This exercise will help you to think systematically about challenges and opportunities in each piece. It will also supply you a common language with which to talk to your new boss, peers, and direct reports about what you are going to do and why.

Leading Change

There is no one-size-fits-all approach to leading change. This is why it's important to be clear about the STARS mix. Using the STARS model, Karl was able to recognize the clear differences between the realignment situation he was heading into (where problems were gradually mounting, but there was no crisis to drive action) and the dramatic turnaround he had successfully managed in Europe (where urgent needs demanded rapid, radical surgery), and he identified the associated implications for how he needed to lead change and manage himself. If Karl had treated

TABLE 3-2

Diagnosing your STARS portfolio

Use the table to identify the mix of STARS situations you face. First, identify which elements (projects, processes, products, perhaps even complete businesses) in your new responsibilities fall into the various STARS situations in the first column; list those elements in the second column. You need not have something in every category. Everything may be in turnaround, or it may be a mix of two or three types. Then use the third column to estimate the percentage of your effort that should be allocated to each category in the next 90 days, making sure it adds up to 100%. Finally, think about which of these situations you most prefer to do. If you also assigned that situation the highest priority, be sure that your preferences are not overly influencing your priorities.

STARS situation	Job element	Priority percentage
Start-up		
Turnaround		
Accelerating growth		
Realignment		
Sustaining success		
		100

his new situation as a turnaround and tried to conduct radical surgery, he probably would have incurred both active and passive resistance, undermining his ability to realize needed change, especially because he was an outsider and therefore vulnerable to being isolated and undercut. Recognizing what was required in North American operations, Karl adopted a more measured approach.

Armed with insight into your STARS portfolio and the key challenges and opportunities, you will adopt the right strategies for leading change. Doing so means, however, adopting the approaches laid out in this book for creating momentum in your next 90 days. Specifically, you must establish priorities, define strategic intent, identify where you can secure early wins, build the right leadership team, and create supporting alliances. Let's look at what Karl did differently in the turnaround and realignment situations he faced.

The starting point, of course, was focused learning. In the turnaround situation in Europe, Karl needed to rapidly assess the organization's technical dimensions—strategy, competitors, products, markets, and technologies—much as a consultant would. In his new leadership role in North America, Karl's learning challenge was markedly different. Technical comprehension was still important, obviously, but cultural and political learning mattered more. That's because internal social dynamics often cause successful organizations to drift into trouble, and because getting people to acknowledge the need for change is much more a political challenge than a technical one. Particularly for a newcomer to the organization, as Karl was, a deep understanding of the culture and politics is a prerequisite for leadership success—and even survival.

Likewise, as Karl worked to establish priorities, he had to weigh the demands of the situation. The European turnaround required radical surgery. The strategy and organizational structure of the business were preventing it from achieving its goals and had to be changed quickly. So Karl closed plants, shifted production, and cut the workforce dramatically. He also rapidly centralized important manufacturing functions in order to reduce fragmentation and cut costs. The North American realignment, in contrast, didn't call for an immediate transformation of strategy or structure. There weren't any major capacity or productivity problems, so plant closures weren't necessary. The manufacturing functions were already centralized and strong. The real problems lay in systems, skills, and culture. It therefore made sense for Karl to focus on those areas.

Situational factors also played a large role in how Karl built his leadership teams in the two situations. To expeditiously turn around the European business, Karl cleaned house at the top of the organization and recruited most of the new senior talent from the outside. In North America, however, the leadership team he inherited was already quite strong. Still, he realized he needed to make a few high-payoff changes in the roster. A couple of central manufacturing roles required leaders with stronger technical skills to support the systems changes he planned to make, and there was an influential manager who, despite Karl's best efforts, didn't grasp the need for change; in fact, the manager's inaction threatened to undermine Karl's leadership. That person's departure sent a crucial message to the rest of the organization. Meanwhile, Karl promoted from within to fill that role and others, and that helped rally the organization behind his plans. People came to see that he wasn't only focusing on the weaknesses of the business but was also appreciative of its strengths.

Finally, Karl had the good judgment to secure early wins differently in the two situations. In turnarounds, leaders must move people out of a state of despair. Karl did that in Europe by closing ailing plants and shifting production, actions that refocused the organization on its core strengths and helped cut unnecessary projects and initiatives. In the realignment, in contrast, Karl's most important early win was to raise people's awareness of the need for change. He accomplished that by putting more emphasis on facts and figures; he revamped the company's performance metrics in manufacturing and customer service to focus employees' attention on critical weaknesses in those areas, and he also introduced external benchmarks and hard-nosed assessments by respected consultants—drawing on impartial voices from outside the company to help make his case. These actions enabled him to pierce the unfounded optimism and send an important message to the rest of the organization.

Key differences between leading change in turnaround and realignment situations are summarized in table 3-3.

TABLE 3-3

Leading change in turnarounds versus realignments

	Turnarounds	Realignments
1. Organize to learn Figure out what you most need to learn, from whom, and how you can best learn it.	Focus on technical learning (strategy, markets, technologies, and so on). Prepare to act quickly.	Focus on cultural and political learning. Prepare to act deliberately.
2. Define strategic intent Develop and communicate a compelling vision for what the organization will become. Outline a clear strategy for achieving that vision.	Prune noncore businesses.	Hone and leverage existing capabilities. Stimulate innovation.
3. Establish A-item priorities Identify a few vital goals and pursue them relentlessly. Think about what you need to have accomplished by the end of year 1 in the new position.	Make faster, bolder moves. Focus on strategy and structure.	Make slower, more deliberate moves. Focus on systems, skills, and culture.
4. Build the leadership team Evaluate the team you inherited. Move deftly to make the necessary changes; find the optimal balance between bringing in outside talent and elevating high potentials within the organization.	Clean house at the top. Recruit external talent.	Make a few important changes. Promote high potentials from within.
5. Secure early wins Think through how you plan to "arrive" in the new organization. Find ways to build personal credibility and energize the ranks.	Shift the organizational mind-set from despair to hope.	Shift the organizational mind-set from denial to awareness.
6. Create supporting alliances Identify how the organization really works and who has influence. Create key coalitions in support of your initiatives.	Gain support from bosses and other stakeholders to invest the required resources.	Build alliances sideways and down to ensure better execution.

Managing Yourself

The STARS state of your organization also has implications for the adjustments you'll need to make to manage yourself. This is particularly true when it comes to determining leadership styles and figuring out whether you are reflexively a "hero" or a "steward."

In turnarounds, leaders are often dealing with people who are hungry for hope, vision, and direction, and that necessitates a heroic style of leadership—charging against the enemy, sword in hand. People line up behind the hero in times of trouble and follow commands. The premium is on rapid diagnosis of the business situation (markets, technologies, products, strategies) and then aggressive moves to cut back the organization to a defensible core. You need to act quickly and decisively, often on the basis of incomplete information.

Clearly, this was the case for Karl in Europe. He immediately took charge, diagnosed the situation, set direction, and made painful calls. Because the outlook was bleak, people were willing to act on his directives without offering much resistance.

Realignments, in contrast, demand from leaders something more akin to stewardship or servant leadership—a more diplomatic and less ego-driven approach that entails building consensus for the need for change. More subtle influence skills come into play; skilled stewards have deep understandings of the culture and politics of their organizations. Stewards are more patient and systematic than heroes in deciding which people, processes, and other resources to preserve and which to discard. They also painstakingly cultivate awareness of the need for change by promoting shared diagnosis, influencing opinion leaders, and encouraging benchmarking.

In his North America appointment, Karl needed to learn to temper some of his heroic tendencies; he had to make careful assessments, move deliberately toward change, and lay a foundation for sustainable success. Whether any leader in transition can adapt her personal leadership strategy successfully depends greatly on the ability to embrace the following pillars of self-management: enhancing self-awareness, exercising personal discipline, and building complementary teams.

Because of their differing imperatives, it is easy for heroes to stumble in realignment and sustaining-success situations and for stewards to struggle in start-ups and turnarounds. The experienced turnaround person facing a realignment is at risk of moving too fast, needlessly causing resistance. The experienced realignment person in a turnaround situation is at risk of moving too slowly and expending energy on cultivating consensus when it is unnecessary to do so, thus squandering precious time.

This is not to say that people who are natural heroes cannot get in touch with their inner stewards and vice versa. Good leaders can succeed in all five of the STARS situations, although no one is equally good at all of them. It is essential to make a hard-headed assessment of which of your skills and inclinations will serve you well in your particular situation and which are likely to get you into trouble. Don't arrive ready for war if what you need is to build alliances.

You also need to remember that leadership is a team sport. Your STARS portfolio has implications for the precise mix of heroes and stewards (every organization needs both) on your leadership team. Karl willed himself toward stewardship in North America, but he knew he more naturally and effectively played the hero role. The implications of this bit of self-awareness were threefold. First, he needed to stock his team with some natural stewards to whom he could turn for wise counsel (lest he go off half-cocked) and to whom he could delegate some of the necessary outreach. Second, he had to identify where it actually made sense to focus some of his heroic energies. After all, every organization, even the most successful, has parts that are in serious trouble. As long as he didn't start setting fires just to fight them and didn't jeopardize the larger goal of realigning the business, this was an appropriate way to achieve a balance. Third, Karl needed to take into consideration STARS preferences and abilities as he hired, promoted, and assigned people to key projects.

Rewarding Success

The STARS framework has implications for how you should evaluate the people who work for you, and for the culture you want to create. Data from the *Harvard Business Review* Transition Survey helps illustrate this essential point. Participants were asked which of the STARS situations they thought were most challenging and in which they would most prefer to be. The results, summarized in table 3-4, are illuminating. The most challenging situation was assessed to be realignment, followed by sustaining success and turnaround. Start-up and accelerated growth were assessed as being significantly easier. However, when it came to preferences, the pattern reversed, with start-up being (by far) the most popular, followed by turnaround and accelerated growth.

This is not a surprising finding, and the underlying reasons are revealing. It is not the case that people are drawn to the easy situations. Rather, they are drawn to situations that are (1) more fun and (2) get more recognition.

A successful start-up is a visible and easily measurable individual accomplishment, as is a successful turnaround. In a realignment, in contrast, success consists of avoiding disaster. It is hard to measure results in a realignment when success means that nothing much happens; it's the dog that doesn't bark. Also, success in realignment requires painstakingly building awareness of the need for change, and

TABLE 3-4

STARS challenges and preferences

Survey respondents were asked to identify which STARS situation they thought was the most challenging and which they most preferred (i.e., would choose if they could). The differences in their assessments are striking, particularly when the sums of the numbers for more action-oriented, authority-driven STARS situations (start-up, turnaround, and accelerated growth) are compared to those that call for more focus on learning, reflection, and influence (realignment and sustaining success).

STARS situation	Most challenging	Most preferred
Start-up	13.5%	47.1%
Turnaround	21.9%	16.7%
Accelerated growth	11.6%	16.1%
Realignment	30.3%	12.7%
Sustaining success	22.6%	7.4%
Total	100%	100%
Start-up, turnaround, or accelerated growth	47.1%	79.9%
Realignment or sustaining success	52.9%	20.1%

that often means giving credit to the group rather than taking it yourself. As for rewarding sustaining success, people seldom call their local power company to say, "Thanks for keeping the lights on today." But if the power goes off, the screaming is immediate and loud.

There is a paradox inherent in rewarding people lavishly for successfully turning around failing businesses (or starting exciting new ventures). Few high-potential leaders show much interest in realignments, preferring the action and recognition associated with turnarounds (and start-ups). So who exactly is responsible for preventing businesses from becoming turnarounds? And does the fact that companies reward turnarounds (and do not know how to reward realignments) make it more likely that businesses will end in crisis? Skilled managers can seemingly count on less-accomplished people to mess up businesses so that they can come charging to the rescue.

The more general point, of course, is that performance must be evaluated and rewarded differently in the different STARS situations. The performance of people put in charge of start-ups and turnarounds is easiest to evaluate, because you can focus on measurable outcomes relative to a clear prior baseline.

Evaluating success and failure in realignment and sustaining-success situations is much more problematic. Performance in a realignment may be better than expected, but still poor. Or it may be that nothing much seems to happen, because a crisis was avoided. Sustaining-success situations pose similar problems. Success may consist of a small loss of market share in the face of a concerted attack by competitors or the eking out of a few percentage points of top-line growth in a mature business. The unknown in both realignments and sustaining-success situations is what would have happened if other actions had been taken or other people had been in charge—the "as compared to what?" problem. Measuring success in such situations takes much more work, because to assess the adequacy of their responses, you must have a deep understanding of the challenges new leaders face and the actions they are taking.

Closing the Loop

Your understanding of the mix of STARS situations inevitably will deepen and shift as you learn more about your new organization. Plan to return to this chapter periodically to reassess your diagnosis of your organization, and think about the implications for what needs to be done and who needs to do it.

MATCH STRATEGY TO SITUATION—CHECKLIST

1. What portfolio of STARS situations have you inherited? Which portions of your responsibilities are in start-up, turnaround, accelerated-growth, realignment, and sustaining-success modes?

2. What are the implications for the challenges and opportunities you are likely to confront, and for the way you should approach accelerating your transition?

3. What are the implications for your learning agenda? Do you need to understand only the technical side of the business, or is it critical that you understand culture and politics as well?

4. What is the prevailing climate in your organization? What psychological transformations do you need to make, and how will you bring them about?

5. How can you best lead change given the situations you face?

6. Which of your skills and strengths are likely to be most valuable in your new situation, and which have the potential to get you into trouble?

7. What are the implications for the team you need to build?

CHAPTER 4

Negotiate Success

When Michael Chen was promoted to be chief information officer for a key business unit of a midsized oil company, he was elated—until he received calls from two colleagues. Both told him the same thing: "Start updating your résumé. Cates is going to eat you alive."

His new boss, Vaughan Cates, was a hard-driving business unit leader with a reputation for getting results—and for being tough on people. She had recently taken over the unit, and several of the people she had inherited had already left.

Michael's friends anticipated the problem. "You've had a lot of success," one said. "But Cates will think you're not aggressive enough. You're a planner and team builder. She'll think you're too slow and not up to the tough decisions."

Forewarned, Michael laid the groundwork with Vaughan to gain time for diagnosis and planning. "I want to operate on a 90-day time frame, starting with 30 days to get on top of things," he told her. "Then I will bring you a detailed assessment and plan with goals and actions for the next 60 days." Michael updated her regularly on his progress. Pressed by her to make a call on a major systems purchase after three weeks, Michael held firm to his schedule. At the end of 30 days, he delivered a strong plan that pleased his new boss.

A month later, Michael returned to report some early wins and to ask Vaughan for more head count to advance a key project. She subjected him to withering questioning, but he was on top of his business case. Eventually she agreed to his requests but set strict deadlines for achieving results. Armed with what he needed, Michael was soon able to report that he had met several interim targets.

Building on his momentum, Michael raised the question of style at their next meeting: "We have different styles, but I can deliver for you," he said. "I want you to judge me on my results, not on how I get them." It took nearly a year, but Michael built a solid, productive working relationship with Vaughan.

To succeed as Michael did with a new boss, it's wise to negotiate success. It's well worth investing time in this critical relationship up front, because your new boss sets your benchmarks, interprets your actions for other key players, and controls access to resources you need. He will have more impact than any other individual on how quickly you reach the break-even point, and on your eventual success or failure.

Negotiating success means proactively engaging with your new boss to shape the game so that you have a fighting chance of achieving desired goals. Many new leaders just play the game, reactively taking their situation as given—and failing as a result. The alternative is to shape the game by negotiating with your boss to establish realistic expectations, reach consensus, and secure sufficient resources. By negotiating effectively with Vaughan, Michael laid the foundation for his success.

Keep in mind that the nature of your relationship with your new boss should depend on your level in the organization and the business situation you face. The higher you rise, the more autonomy you're likely to have. This is especially the case if you and your boss are situated in different locations. Lack of oversight can be a blessing if you get what you need to succeed. Or it can be a curse if you get enough rope to hang yourself.

What you need from a boss also varies among the STARS business situations. In start-ups, you need resources and perhaps protection from higher-level interference. In turnarounds, you may need to be pushed to cut back the business quickly to the defensible core. When you're accelerating growth, the key may be securing appropriate levels of investment. If you're in a realignment, you may need your boss to help you make the case for change. In a sustaining-success situation, you may need help to learn about the business and avoid early mistakes that threaten the core assets.

There is much you can do to build a productive working relationship with your new boss, and you should start doing it as soon as you're being considered for a new role. Keep it in mind as you participate in interviews, get selected, and formally begin the new job.

This chapter shows you how to engage in the right kinds of dialogue with your new boss. Read it even if you will be reporting to the same boss in your new role. Your relationship likely won't stay the same. The boss's expectations may be different, and you may need more resources. Many managers mistakenly assume that they can continue to work with a current boss in the same way despite being in a different role. Don't make this error.

Think also about how you might use the ideas in this chapter to accelerate relationship building with your own new direct reports. After all, don't you have a big stake in getting them to the break-even point as quickly as possible?

Focusing on the Fundamentals

How do you build a productive relationship with a new boss? There are some basic do's and don'ts. Let's start with the don'ts.

- **Don't stay away.** If you have a boss who doesn't reach out to you, or with whom you have uncomfortable interactions, you will have to reach out yourself. Otherwise, you risk potentially crippling communication gaps. It may feel good to be given a lot of rope, but resist the urge to take it. Get on your boss's calendar regularly. Be sure your boss is aware of the issues you face and that you are aware of her expectations, especially whether and how they're shifting.

- **Don't surprise your boss.** It's no fun bringing your boss bad news. However, most bosses consider it a far greater sin not to report emerging problems early enough. Worst of all is for your boss to learn about a problem from someone else. It's usually best to give your new boss at least a heads-up as soon as you become aware of a developing problem.

- **Don't approach your boss only with problems.** That said, you don't want to be perceived as bringing nothing but problems for your boss to solve. You also need to have plans for how you will proceed.

This emphatically does not mean that you must fashion full-blown solutions: the outlay of time and effort to generate solutions can easily lure you down the rocky road to surprising your boss. The key here is to give some thought to how to address the problem—even if it is only gathering more information—and to your role and the help you will need. (This is a good thing to keep in mind in dealing with direct reports, too. It can be dangerous to say, "Don't bring me problems, bring me solutions." Far better is, "Don't just bring me problems, bring me plans for how we can begin to address them.")

- **Don't run down your checklist.** There is a tendency, even for senior leaders, to use meetings with a boss as an opportunity to run through your checklist of what you've been doing. Sometimes this is appropriate, but it is rarely what your boss needs or wants to hear. You should assume she wants to focus on the most important things you're trying to do and how she can help. Don't go in without at most three things you really need to share or on which you need action.

- **Don't expect your boss to change.** You and your new boss may have very different working styles. You may communicate in different ways, motivate in different ways, and prefer different levels of detail in overseeing your direct reports. But it's your responsibility to adapt to your boss's style; you need to adapt your approach to work with your boss's preferences.

There are some fundamental do's as well. Following them will make your life easier.

- **Clarify expectations early and often.** Begin managing expectations from the moment you consider taking a new role. Focus on expectations during the interview process. You are in trouble if your boss expects you to fix things fast when you know the business has serious structural problems. It's wise to get bad news on the table early and to lower unrealistic expectations. Then check in regularly to make sure your boss's expectations have not shifted. Revisiting expectations is especially important if you're onboarding from the outside and don't have a deep understanding of the culture and politics.

- **Take 100 percent responsibility for making the relationship work.** This is the flip side of "Don't stay away." Don't expect your boss to reach out or to offer you the time and support you need. It's best to begin by assuming that it's on your shoulders to make the relationship work. If your boss meets you partway, it will be a welcome surprise.

- **Negotiate time lines for diagnosis and action planning.** Don't let yourself get caught up immediately in firefighting or be pressured to make calls before you're ready. Buy yourself some time, even if it's only a few weeks, to diagnose the new organization and come up with an action plan. It worked for Michael in his dealings with Vaughan, and it can work for you. The 90-day plan discussed at the end of this chapter is an excellent vehicle.

- **Aim for early wins in areas important to the boss.** Whatever your own priorities, figure out what your boss cares about most. What are his priorities and goals, and how do your actions fit into this picture? Once you know, aim for early results in those areas. One good way is to focus on three things that are important to your boss and discuss what you're doing about them every time you interact. In that way, your boss will feel ownership of your success.

- **Pursue good marks from those whose opinions your boss respects.** Your new boss's opinion of you will be based in part on direct interactions and in part on what she hears about you from trusted others. Your boss will have preexisting relationships with people who are now your peers and possibly your subordinates. You needn't curry favor with the people your boss trusts. Simply be alert to the multiple channels through which information and opinion about you will reach your boss.

With these basic rules in mind, you can begin to plan how to engage with your new boss.

Planning for Five Conversations

Your relationship with your new boss will be built through an ongoing dialogue. Your discussions will begin before you accept the new position and continue into your transition and beyond. Several fundamental subjects belong at the center of this dialogue. In fact, it's valuable to include plans for five specific conversations with your new boss about transition-related subjects in your 90-day plan. These are not subjects to be dealt with in separate meetings but are intertwined threads of dialogue.

1. **The situational diagnosis conversation.** In this conversation, you seek to understand how your new boss sees the

STARS portfolio you have inherited. Are there elements of start-up, turnaround, accelerated growth, realignment, and sustaining success? How did the organization reach this point? What factors—both soft and hard—make this situation a challenge? What resources within the organization can you draw on? Your view may differ from your boss's, but it is essential to grasp how she sees the situation.

2. **The expectations conversation.** Your goal in this conversation is to understand and negotiate expectations. What does your new boss need you to do in the short term and in the medium term? What will constitute success? Critically, how will your performance be measured? When? You might conclude that your boss's expectations are unrealistic and that you need to work to reset them. Also, as part of your broader campaign to secure early wins, discussed in the next chapter, keep in mind that it's better to underpromise and overdeliver.

3. **The resource conversation.** This conversation is essentially a negotiation for critical resources. What do you need to be successful? What do you need your boss to do? The resources need not be limited to funding or personnel. In a realignment, for example, you may need help from your boss to persuade the organization to confront the need for change. Key here is to focus your boss on the benefits and costs of what you can accomplish with different amounts of resources.

4. **The style conversation.** This conversation is about how you and your new boss can best interact on an ongoing basis. What forms of communication does he prefer, and for what? Face-to-face? Voice, electronic? How often?

What kinds of decisions does he want to be consulted on, and when can you make the call on your own? How do your styles differ, and what are the implications for the ways you should interact?

5. **The personal development conversation.** Once you're a few months into your new role, you can begin to discuss how you're doing and what your developmental priorities should be. Where are you doing well? In what areas do you need to improve or do things differently? Are there projects or special assignments you could undertake (without sacrificing focus)?

In practice, your dialogue about these subjects will overlap and evolve over time. You might address several of the five issues in a single meeting, or you might work out issues related to one subject through a series of brief exchanges. Michael covered style and expectations in a single meeting and established a schedule for talking about the situation and more deeply about expectations.

However, there is logic to the sequence just described. Your early conversations should focus on situational diagnosis, expectations, and style. As you learn more, you will be ready to negotiate for resources, revisiting your diagnosis of the situation and resetting expectations as necessary. When you feel the relationship is reasonably well established, you can introduce the personal development conversation. Take time to plan for each conversation, and signal clearly to your boss what you hope to accomplish in each exchange.

Use table 4-1 to take stock of where you currently stand in having each of these conversations and what your priorities are for the next 30 days. If you're in the process of interviewing for a new role, use it to capture what you've learned and identify focal points for conversation.

TABLE 4-1

The five conversations

Conversation	Current status	Priorities for the next 30 days
Situation: How does your boss see your STARS portfolio?		
Expectations: What are you expected to accomplish?		
Resources: What resources do you have at your disposal?		
Style: How can you best work together?		
Personal development: What is going well, and what do you need to do differently?		

Now use the detailed guidelines that follow to plan the next steps for each of the five conversations with your new boss.

Planning the Situation Conversation

Reaching a shared understanding of the business situation you face, and of its associated challenges and opportunities, is your goal in the *situational diagnosis* conversation. This shared understanding is the foundation for everything you will do. If you and your boss do not define your new situation in the same way, you will not receive the support you need. Thus, your first discussion should center on clearly defining your new situation using the STARS model as a shared language. (The same is true, as I discuss later, with your team.)

Match Your Support to Your Situation

The support you need from your boss will depend on your STARS portfolio—start-up, turnaround, accelerated growth, realignment, sustaining success, or some mix. Once you reach a common understanding of the situation, think carefully about the role you need your new boss to play and the kinds of support you will ask for. In all five situations, you need your boss to give you the direction, support, and space to do your job. Table 4-2 lists typical roles your boss might play in each of the STARS situations.

TABLE 4-2

Matching support to your situation

Situation	Typical roles for your boss
Start-up	• Help getting needed resources quickly • Clear, measurable goals • Guidance at strategic breakpoints • Help staying focused
Turnaround	Same as start-up, plus • Support for making tough personnel calls • Support for changing or correcting external image • Help cutting deeply enough, fast enough
Accelerated growth	Same as start-up, plus • Support for getting investment to fuel growth at the right rate in the right ways • Help making the case for new systems and structures
Realignment	Same as start-up, plus • Help making the case for change, especially if you're from outside
Sustaining success	Same as start-up, plus • Constant reality testing: Is this a sustaining-success situation, or is it a realignment? • Support for playing good defense and avoiding mistakes that damage the business • Help finding ways to take the business to a new level

Planning the Expectations Conversation

The point of the *expectations* conversation is for you and your boss to clarify and align your expectations about the future. You need to agree on short- and medium-term goals and on timing. Critically, you need to agree on how your boss will measure progress. What will constitute success, for your boss and for you? When does your boss expect to see results? How will you measure success? Over what time frame? If you succeed, what is next? If you don't manage expectations, they will manage you.

Match Expectations to the Situation

Closely align your expectations with your shared assessment of the situation. In a turnaround situation, for example, you and your boss would probably agree on the need to take decisive action quickly. You would both have explicit expectations for the immediate future, such as making difficult decisions to reduce costs in nonessential areas or concentrating on the products with the highest margins. In this scenario, you would probably measure success by improvements in the business's overall financial performance.

Aim for Early Wins in Areas Important to Your Boss

Whatever your own priorities, pinpoint what your boss cares about most, and aim for early wins in those areas. If you want to succeed, you need your boss's help; in turn, you should help her succeed. When you pay attention to your boss's priorities, she will feel ownership in your success. The most effective approach is to integrate your boss's goals with your own efforts to get early wins. If this is impossible, look for early wins based solely on your boss's priorities.

Identify the Untouchables

If there are parts of the organization—products, facilities, people—about which your new boss is proprietary, it is essential to identify them as soon as possible. You don't want to find out that you're pressing to shut down the product line your boss started up or to replace someone who has been his loyal ally. So try to deduce what your boss is sensitive about. You can do this by understanding your boss's personal history, by talking to others, and by paying close attention to facial expression, tone, and body language. If you're uncertain, float an idea gently as a trial balloon, and then watch his reactions closely.

Educate Your Boss

One of your immediate tasks is to shape your boss's perceptions of what you can and should achieve. You may find her expectations unrealistic, or simply at odds with your own beliefs about what needs to be done. If so, you must work hard to make your views converge. In a realignment, for example, your boss might attribute the worst problems to a certain part of the business, whereas you believe they lie elsewhere. In this case, you would need to educate your boss about the underlying problems to reset expectations. Proceed carefully—especially if your boss feels invested in the way things have always been or is responsible in part for the problems.

Underpromise and Overdeliver

Whether you and your boss agree on expectations, try to bias yourself somewhat toward underpromising achievements and overdelivering results. This strategy contributes to building credibility. Consider how your organization's capacity for change might affect your ability to deliver on the promises you make.

Be conservative in what you promise. If you deliver more, you will delight your boss. But if you promise too much and fail to deliver, you risk undermining your credibility. Even if you accomplish a great deal, you will have failed in the boss's eyes.

Clarify, Clarify, Clarify

Even if you're sure you know what your boss expects, you should go back regularly to confirm and clarify. Some bosses know what they want but are not good at expressing it. You don't want to achieve clarity only after you have headed down the wrong road. So you must be prepared to keep asking questions until you're sure you understand. Try, for example, asking the same questions in different ways to gain more insight. Work at reading between the lines accurately and developing good hypotheses about what your boss is likely to want. Try to put yourself in his shoes and understand how his boss will evaluate him. Figure out how you fit into the larger picture. Above all, don't let key issues remain ambiguous. Ambiguity about goals and expectations is dangerous. A tie in a conflict over what was said about expectations in an earlier conversation doesn't go to you. It goes to your boss.

Planning the Resource Conversation

The *resource* conversation is an ongoing negotiation with your new boss for critical resources. Before you launch this conversation, you must have agreement with your boss on your STARS portfolio and associated goals and expectations. Now you must secure the resources you need to meet those expectations.

The resources you need will depend on the situations you're dealing with.

- In start-up situations, your most urgent needs are likely to be adequate financial resources, technical support, and people with the right expertise.

- In turnaround situations, you need authority, backed by political support, to make the tough decisions and secure scarce financial and human resources.

- In accelerated-growth situations, you need the investment necessary to support growth, as well as support for putting in place needed systems and structures.

- In realignment situations, you need consistent, public backing to get the organization to confront the need for change. Ideally, your boss will stand shoulder to shoulder with you, helping pierce through denial and complacency.

- In sustaining-success situations, you require financial and technical resources to sustain the core business and exploit promising new opportunities. You also need periodic pushes to set stretch goals that will keep you from drifting into complacency.

The first step is to decide what resources—tangible and intangible—you must have to succeed. Identify the resources already available to you, such as experienced people or new products ready to be launched. Then identify the resources you will need help in obtaining. Ask yourself, "What exactly do I need from my boss?" The sooner you can articulate the resources you need, the sooner you can broach these requests.

It's best to put as much as possible on the table as early as possible. Try using the menu approach: lay out the costs and benefits of different levels of resource commitment. "If you want my sales to grow seven percent next year, I need investment of X dollars. If you want ten percent growth, I will need Y dollars." Going back for more too often is a sure way to lose credibility. If it takes more time to get a handle on the resources you need to achieve specific goals, then so be it. Michael negotiated for the necessary time—a critical resource—to avoid this problem.

Play or Change the Game?

You may be able to achieve your goals by playing the game according to the prevailing rules. If you can maneuver within the accepted cultural and political norms, your resource requests will be expected—and you will find it easier to get what you need.

In other situations—notably realignments and turnarounds—you may need to change or even abandon established ways of doing business. Your resource requests will probably be more sweeping, and failure to secure them more damaging. You will have to negotiate harder to get what you need. These circumstances call for being clear about how the situation, expectations, and resources must line up to give you a reasonable shot at success. Clarify your needs in your own mind before you enter these discussions, back them up with as much hard data as you can get, and prepare to explain exactly why you see certain resources as essential. Then stick to your guns. Keep coming back. Enlist others to help make your case. Seek out allies within and outside your organization. It is better to push too hard than to slowly bleed to death.

Negotiate for Resources

As you seek commitments for resources, keep these principles of effective negotiation in mind.

- **Focus on underlying interests.** Probe as deeply as possible to understand the agendas of your boss and any others from whom you need to secure resources. What is in it for them?

- **Look for mutually beneficial exchanges.** Seek resources that both support your boss's agenda and advance your own. Look for ways to help peers advance their agendas in return for help with yours.

- **Link resources to results.** Highlight the performance benefits that will result if more resources are dedicated to your unit. Create the menu described earlier, laying out what you can achieve (and cannot achieve) with current resources and what different-sized increments would allow you to do.

Planning the Style Conversation

People's stylistic preferences affect how they learn, communicate, influence others, and make decisions. In the *style* conversation, your agenda is to determine how you and your boss can best work together on a continuing basis. This was the key challenge that Michael faced in working out his relationship with Vaughan. Even if your boss never becomes a close friend or mentor, it's essential that you understand what it takes to build a productive working relationship.

Diagnose Your Boss's Style

The first step is to diagnose your new boss's working style and figure out how it jibes with your own. If you leave messages for her about an urgent problem, and she doesn't respond quickly but then reproaches you for not giving her a heads-up about the problem, take note: your boss doesn't use that mode of communication!

How does your boss like to communicate? How often? What kinds of decisions does he want to be involved in, and when can you make calls on your own? Does your boss arrive at the office early and work late? Does he expect others to do the same?

Pinpoint the specific ways in which your styles differ, and assess what those differences imply about how you will interact. Suppose you prefer to learn by talking with knowledgeable people, whereas your boss relies more on reading and analyzing hard data. What kinds of misunderstandings and problems might this difference in style cause, and how can you avoid them? Or suppose your new boss tends to micromanage, but you prefer a lot of independence. What can you do to manage this tension?

You may find it helpful to talk to others who have worked with your boss in the past. Naturally, you must do this judiciously. Be careful not to be perceived as eliciting criticism of how the boss leads. Stick to less fraught issues, such as how the boss prefers to communicate. Listen to others' perspectives, but base your evolving strategy chiefly on your own experience.

Observe, too, how your boss deals with others. Is there consistency? If not, why not? Does the boss have favorites? Is he particularly prone to micromanaging certain issues? Has he come down hard on a few people because of unacceptable performance?

Scope Out the Dimensions of Your Box

Your boss will have a comfort zone about her involvement in decision making. Think of this zone as defining the boundaries of the decision-making box in which you will operate. What sorts of decisions does she want you to make on your own but tell her about? Are you free, for example, to make key personnel decisions? When does she want to be consulted before you decide? Is it when your actions touch on broader issues of policy—for example, in granting people leave? Or when there are hot political issues associated with some of the projects you're working on? When does she want to make the decision herself?

Initially, expect to be confined to a relatively small box. As your new boss gains confidence in you, the dimensions of the box should increase. If not, or if it remains too small to allow you to be effective, you may have to address the issue directly.

Adapt to Your Boss's Style

Assume that the job of building a positive relationship with your new boss is 100 percent your responsibility. In short, this means adapting to his style. If your boss hates voice messages, don't leave them. If he wants to know in detail what is going on, over-communicate. Of course you should not do anything that could compromise your ability to achieve superior business results, but do look for opportunities to smooth the day-to-day workings of your relationship. Others who have worked with your boss can tell you what approaches they found successful. Then judiciously experiment with the tactics that seem most promising in your case. When in doubt, simply ask your boss how he would prefer you to proceed.

Surface the Difficult Issues

When serious style differences arise, it's best to address them directly. Otherwise, you run the risk that your boss will interpret a style difference as disrespect or even incompetence on your part.

Raise the style issue before it becomes a source of irritation, and talk with your boss about how to accommodate both your styles. This conversation can smooth the path for both of you to achieve your goals. This is what Michael did, although he wisely waited to build credibility before addressing it.

One proven strategy is to focus your early conversations on goals and results instead of how you achieve them. You might simply say that you expect to notice differences in how the two of you approach certain issues or decisions but that you're committed to achieving the results to which you have both agreed. An assertion of this kind prepares your boss to expect differences. You may have to remind your boss periodically to focus on the results you're achieving and not on your methods.

It may also help to judiciously discuss style issues with someone your boss trusts, who can enlighten you about potential issues and solutions before you raise them directly with your boss. If you find the right adviser, he may even help you broach a difficult issue in a nonthreatening manner.

Don't make the mistake of trying to address all style issues in a single conversation. Nevertheless, an early dialogue explicitly devoted to style is an excellent place to start. Expect to continue to be attentive to, and adapt to, the boss's style as your relationship evolves.

Planning the Personal Development Conversation

Finally, when your relationship with your boss has matured a bit (roughly the 90-day mark is a good rule of thumb), begin to discuss how you're doing. This need not be a formal performance review, but it does need to be an open discussion of how things are going. What are you doing well, and what do you need to do differently? What skills do you need to develop to do the job better? Are there shortcomings in your leadership capacities that you need to address? Are there projects or special assignments that you could get involved in (without sacrificing focus) that could strengthen your skills?

It's especially critical that you do this when you're making key career passages. If you're a first-time manager, get into the habit early of asking your boss for feedback and help in developing your supervisory skills. Your willingness to seek candid feedback on your strengths and weaknesses—and, critically, your ability to act on the feedback—sends a powerful message.

The same principle holds whether you're becoming a manager of managers for the first time, a functional leader, a general manager, or a CEO. Whenever you are at a point in your career when success demands a different set of skills and attitudes, discipline yourself to be open to learning from others who have gone before you.

Don't restrict your focus to hard skills. The higher you rise, the more important the key soft skills of cultural and political diagnosis, negotiation, coalition building, and conflict management will become. Formal training can help, but developmental assignments—in project teams, in new parts of the organization, in different functions, in different locations—are indispensable in honing these key managerial skills.

Working with Multiple Bosses

You face even more daunting challenges in managing expectations if you have more than one boss (direct or dotted-line). The same principles hold, but the emphasis shifts. If you have multiple bosses, you must be sure to carefully balance perceived wins and losses among them. If one boss has substantially more power, then it makes sense to bias yourself somewhat in her direction early on, as long as you redress the balance, to the greatest extent possible, later. If you can't get agreement by working with your bosses one-on-one, you must essentially force them to come to the table together to thrash issues out. Otherwise, you will get pulled to pieces. You should complete a version of table 4-1 for each of your bosses, and look closely at where their views of the situations, expectations, and resources converge and where they diverge. Pay attention, too, to differences in their styles, and adapt accordingly.

Working at a Distance

Managing when you are located far from your boss presents a different set of challenges. The risk is greater of falling out of step without realizing it. This puts the onus on you to exert even more discipline over communication, scheduling calls and meetings to be sure you stay aligned. It also is even more critical to establish clear and comprehensive metrics so that your boss gets a reasonable picture of what is going on and you can more effectively manage by exception.

If it is humanly possible, you should plan to have one or more in-person meetings with your boss early on. It is essential to make face-to-face connections early on to begin to establish a basis of confidence and trust (the same is true if you're leading a virtual team). So if this means you need to fight for the resources and fly halfway around the world, you should do it.

Think, too, about good ways to carve out time with your boss, who is likely to be busy and buffeted by requests from people who are more physically present than you are. Identify windows of time when your boss is less likely to be completely occupied— for example, during the times when she is traveling to or from the office.

Putting It All Together: Negotiating Your 90-Day Plan

No matter what situation you're entering, it can be useful to create a 90-day plan and get buy-in from your boss. Usually, you will be able to devise a plan after a couple of weeks in the new job, when you have begun to connect with the organization and get the lay of the land.

Your 90-day plan should be written, even if it consists only of bullet points. It should specify priorities and goals as well as milestones. Critically, you should share it with your boss and seek buy-in for it. It should serve as a "contract" between the two of you about how you're going to spend your time, spelling out both what you will do and what you will not do.

To begin to sketch out your plan, divide the 90 days into three blocks of 30 days. At the end of each block, you will have a review meeting with your boss. (Naturally, you're likely to interact more often than that.) You should typically devote the first block of 30 days to learning and building personal credibility. Like Michael, you should negotiate for this early learning period and then try to hold your boss to that agreement. Then you can proceed to develop a learning agenda and learning plan for yourself. Set weekly goals for yourself, and establish a personal discipline of weekly evaluation and planning.

Your key outputs at the end of the first 30 days will be a diagnosis of the situation, an identification of key priorities, and a plan for how you will spend the next 30 days. This plan should address where and how you will begin to seek some early wins. Your review meeting with your boss should focus on the situation and expectations conversations, with an eye to reaching consensus about the situation, clarification of expectations, and buy-in to your plan for the next 30 days. Continue the weekly discipline of evaluation and planning.

At the 60-day mark, your review meeting should focus on assessing your progress toward the goals of your plan for the previous 30 days. You should also discuss what you plan to achieve in the next 30 days (that is, by the end of 90 days). Depending on the situation and your level in the organization, your goals at this juncture might include identifying the resources necessary to pursue major initiatives, fleshing out your initial assessments of strategy and structure, and presenting some early assessments of your team.

Planning the Five Conversations with Your Team

Finally, you won't merely *have* a new boss; you are likely to *be* a new boss as well. You will almost certainly have new subordinates. Just as you need to develop a productive relationship with your new boss, so, too, will they need to work effectively with you. In the past, have you done a good job of helping subordinates with their transitions? What might you do differently this time?

Think about how to apply all the advice in this chapter to working with your own direct reports. The golden rule of transitions is to transition others as you would wish to be transitioned yourself (see "The Golden Rule of Transitions"). The same five-conversation framework can help you build productive relationships with the people who report to you. Introduce the framework to them right away, and schedule a first conversation with each of them to talk about the situation and about your expectations. Get them to do some pre-work before the meeting—for example, reading the chapter on matching strategy to situation. See how fast you can accelerate their transitions.

The Golden Rule of Transitions

Think about how you would like new bosses to help you transition into new roles. Ideally, what kinds of guidance and support would they give you? Now think about how you deal with new direct reports. What kinds of guidance and support do you give them?

Now juxtapose these assessments. Do you transition others as you would wish to be transitioned yourself? If there is a big inconsistency between how you prefer to be dealt with as a new direct report and how you deal with new direct reports, then you are part of the problem.

Helping direct reports accelerate their transitions is about more than being a good manager and contributing to others' development. The faster your direct reports get up to speed, the better able they will be to help you reach your goals.

Use table 4-3 to keep track of where you stand in having those key conversations with each of your reports.

TABLE 4-3

The five conversations and your team

*List your team members in the first column. Then assess where you stand
in having the five conversations with each one. Circle the ones that are your
priorities.*

Team member	Situation	Expectations	Resources	Style	Personal development

NEGOTIATE SUCCESS—CHECKLIST

1. How effectively have you built relationships with new
   bosses in the past? What have you done well? Where do
   you need improvement?

2. Create a plan for the situational conversation. Based on
   what you know now, what issues will you raise with your
   boss in this conversation? What do you want to say up
   front? In what order do you want to raise issues?

3. Create a plan for the expectations conversation. How will
   you figure out what your new boss expects you to do?

4. Create a plan for the style conversation. How will you
   figure out how best to work with your boss? What mode

of communication does he prefer? How often should you interact? How much detail should you provide? What types of issues should you consult with him about before deciding?

5. Create a plan for the resource conversation. Given what you need to do, what resources are absolutely needed? With fewer resources, what would you have to forgo? If you had more resources, what would the benefits be? Be sure to build the business case.

6. Create a plan for the personal development conversation. What are your strengths, and where do you need improvement? What kinds of assignments or projects might help you develop skills you need?

7. How might you use the five conversations framework to accelerate the development of your team? Where are you in terms of having the key conversations with each of your direct reports?

CHAPTER 5

Secure Early Wins

When Elena Lee was promoted to head customer service at a leading retailer, she was tasked with improving slumping customer satisfaction. She also was determined to change the authoritarian leadership culture exemplified by her predecessor. Before her promotion, Elena had been responsible for the highest-performing call center in the same organization, so she knew a lot about the problems other units had been facing with quality of service. Convinced that she could dramatically improve performance through more employee participation, she saw cultural change as a top priority.

Elena began by communicating her goals to her former peers, now direct reports—the leaders of the company's call centers across the globe. In a series of team calls and 1:1 meetings, she laid out her quality improvement goals and vision for a more participative, problem-solving culture. These early overtures generated little obvious reaction.

Next, she initiated weekly meetings with each of the call center managers to review unit performance and discuss how they were working to improve it. Elena stressed that "the punishment culture is a thing of the past" and that she expected managers to coach employees. Cases involving significant disciplinary measures, she said, should be referred (on an interim basis) directly to her for review.

Over time Elena learned which center managers were getting with the program and which ones were continuing to be punitive. She then conducted formal performance reviews and put two of the worst offenders on performance-improvement plans. One left almost immediately; she replaced him with a high-potential supervisor from the center she had run. Although it took some time, the other manager shaped up acceptably.

Meanwhile, Elena focused on a critical aspect of the business: evaluation of customer satisfaction and improvement in quality of service. She appointed her best unit leader to lead a team of promising frontline managers and tasked them with producing a plan to introduce new metrics and supporting performance feedback and improvement processes. She also engaged a consultant to advise the managers on how to pursue this project, and she regularly reviewed their progress. When the team presented recommendations, she promptly implemented them on a pilot basis in the unit previously overseen by the departed supervisor.

By the end of her first year, Elena had extended the new approach throughout the organization. Customer service had improved substantially, and climate surveys revealed striking improvements in morale and employee satisfaction.

Elena succeeded in quickly creating momentum and building personal credibility by securing early wins.[1] By the end of the first few months, you want your boss, your peers, and your subordinates to feel that something new, something good, is happening. Early wins excite and energize people and build your personal credibility. Done well, they help you create value for your new organization earlier and reach the break-even point much more quickly.

Making Waves

A seminal study of executives in transition found that they plan and implement change in distinct waves, as illustrated in figure 5-1.[2] Following an early period of focused learning, these leaders begin an early wave of changes. The pace then slows to allow consolidation and deeper learning about the organization, and to allow people to catch their breath. Armed with more insight, these executives then implement deeper waves of change. A final, less extreme wave focuses on fine-tuning to maximize performance. By this point, most of these leaders are ready to move on.

This research has direct implications for how you should manage your transition. It suggests that you should keep your ends clearly in mind when you devise your plan to secure early wins. The transition lasts only a few months, but you typically will

FIGURE 5-1

Waves of change

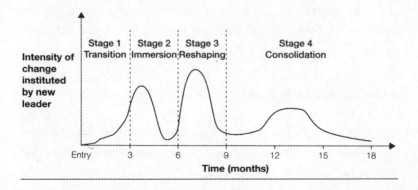

remain in the same job for two to four years before moving on to a new position. To the greatest extent possible, your early wins should advance longer-term goals.

Plan Your Waves

In planning for your transition (and beyond), focus on making successive waves of change. Each wave should consist of distinct phases: learning, designing the changes, building support, implementing the changes, and observing results. Thinking in this way can release you to spend time up front to learn and prepare, and afterward to consolidate and get ready for the next wave. If you keep changing things, it is impossible to figure out what is working and what is not. Unending change is also a surefire recipe for burning out your people.

The goal of the first wave of change is to secure early wins. The new leader tailors early initiatives to build personal credibility, establish key relationships, and identify and harvest low-hanging fruit—the highest-potential opportunities for short-term improvements in organizational performance. Done well, this strategy helps the new leader build momentum and deepen his own learning.

The second wave of change typically addresses more fundamental issues of strategy, structure, systems, and skills to reshape the organization; deeper gains in organizational performance are achieved. But you will not get there if you don't secure early wins in the first wave.

Starting with the Goal

Leaders in transition understandably are eager to get things moving. Thus, they naturally tend to focus on the problems that are easiest to fix quickly. This tactic is fine, up to a point. But be careful not to fall into the *low-hanging fruit trap*. This trap catches leaders when they expend most of their energy seeking early wins that don't contribute to achieving their longer-term business objectives. It's like trying to launch a rocket into orbit with nothing except a very big first stage; the risk is great that you'll fall back to earth once the initial momentum fades. The implication: when you're deciding where to seek early wins, you may have to forgo some of the low-hanging fruit and reach higher in the tree.

As you strive to create momentum, therefore, keep in mind that your early wins must do double duty: they must help you build momentum in the short term *and* lay a foundation for achieving your longer-term business goals. So be sure that your plans for securing early wins, to the greatest extent possible, (1) are consistent with your agreed-to goals—what your bosses and key stakeholders expect you to achieve—and (2) help you introduce the new patterns of behavior you need to achieve those goals.

Focus on Business Priorities

The goals you have agreed to with your boss and other key stakeholders are the destination you're striving to reach in measurable business objectives. Examples are double-digit annual profit growth; a dramatic cut in defects and rework; or completion of a key project by an agreed-to deadline. For Elena, her number 1 priority was to make significant improvements in customer satisfaction. The point is to define your goals so that you can lead with a distinct end point in mind.

Identify and Support Behavioral Changes

Your agreed-to goals are the destination, but the behavior of people in your organization is a key part of how you do (or don't) get there. Put another way, if you are to achieve your goals in the allotted time, you may have to change dysfunctional patterns of behavior.

Start by identifying the unwanted behaviors; for example, Elena wanted to reduce the fear and disempowerment in her organization. Then work out, as Elena did, a clear vision of how you would like people to behave by the end of your tenure in the job, and plan how your actions in pursuit of early wins will advance the process. What behaviors do people consistently display that undermine the potential for high performance? Take a look at table 5-1, which lists some problematic behavior patterns, and then summarize your thoughts about the behaviors you would like to change.

TABLE 5-1

Problematic behavior patterns

Lack of...	Symptoms
Focus	• The group can't clearly define its priorities, or it has too many priorities. • Resources are spread too thin, leading to frequent crises and firefighting. People are rewarded for their ability to put out fires, not for devising enduring solutions.
Discipline	• People exhibit great variation in their levels of performance. • Employees don't understand the negative consequences of inconsistency. • People make excuses when they fail to meet commitments.
Innovation	• The group uses internal benchmarks to measure performance. • Improvements in products and processes unfold slowly and incrementally. • Employees are rewarded for maintaining stable performance, not for pushing the envelope.
Teamwork	• Team members compete with one another and protect turf rather than work together to achieve collective goals. • People are rewarded for creating fiefdoms.
Sense of urgency	• Team members ignore the needs of external and internal customers. • Complacency reigns, revealed in beliefs such as, "We're the best and always have been" and "It doesn't matter if we respond immediately; it won't make any difference."

Adopting Basic Principles

It's crucial to get early wins, but it's also important to secure them in the right way. Above all, of course, you want to avoid early losses, because it's tough to recover once the tide is running against you. Here are some basic principles to consider.

- **Focus on a few promising opportunities.** It's easy to take on too much during a transition, and the results can be ruinous. You cannot hope to achieve results in more than a couple of areas during your transition. Thus, it's essential to identify the most promising opportunities and then focus relentlessly on translating them into wins. Think of it as risk management: pursue enough focal points to have a good shot at getting a significant success, but not so many that your efforts get diffused.

- **Get wins that matter to your boss.** It's essential to get early wins that energize your direct reports and other employees. But your boss's opinion about your accomplishments is crucial too. Even if you do not fully endorse her priorities, you must make them central in thinking through which early wins you will aim for. Addressing problems that your boss cares about will go a long way toward building credibility and cementing your access to resources.

- **Get wins in the right ways.** If you achieve impressive results in a manner that is seen as manipulative, underhanded, or inconsistent with the culture, you're setting yourself up for trouble. If Elena had gotten her key wins by being punitive, it would have undercut the larger objective she was trying to achieve. An early win that is accomplished in a way that exemplifies the behavior you hope to instill in your new organization is a double win.

- **Take your STARS portfolio into account.** What con-
  stitutes an early win differs dramatically from one
  STARS business situation to another. Simply getting
  people to talk about the organization and its challenges
  can be a big accomplishment in a realignment, but it's
  a waste of time in a turnaround. So think hard about
  what will build momentum best in each part of your
  portfolio. Will it be a demonstrated willingness to listen
  and learn? Will it be rapid, decisive calls on pressing
  business issues?

- **Adjust for the culture.** In some organizations, a win
  must be a visible individual accomplishment. In others, individual pursuit of glory, even if it achieves good
  results, is viewed as grandstanding and destructive of
  teamwork. In team-oriented organizations, early wins
  could come in the form of leading a team in the development of a new product idea or being viewed as a solid
  contributor and team player in a broader initiative. Be
  sure you understand what is and is not viewed as a win,
  especially if you're onboarding into the organization.

Identifying Your Early Wins

Armed with (and guided by) an understanding of your goals and
objectives for behavior change, you can identify where you will
seek early wins. You should think about what you need to do
in two phases: building personal credibility in roughly the first
30 days, and deciding which projects you will launch to achieve
early performance improvements beyond that. (The actual time
frames will of course depend on the situation.)

Understand Your Reputation

When you arrive, people will rapidly begin to assess you and your capabilities. In part, this evaluation will be based on what people think they already "know" about you. You can be sure people have talked to people who have talked to people who have worked with you in the past. So like it or not, you will start your role with a reputation, deserved or not. The risk, of course, is that your reputation will become reality, because people tend to focus on information that confirms their beliefs and screen out information that doesn't—the so-called *confirmation bias*.[3] The implication is that you need to figure out what role people are expecting you to play and then make an explicit decision about whether you will reinforce these expectations or confound them.

Elena's situation—leading former peers—is a special case in which people in the organization knew her, but in a different, more junior role. The risk for her was that they would expect her to be the same in her new role. So her job was to figure out ways to change how people perceived her. The broader challenges of leading former peers are summarized in the box "Leading Former Peers."

Leading Former Peers

To meet the classic challenges of moving from peer to boss, you should adopt the following principles:

- **Accept the fact that relationships must change.** An unfortunate price of promotion is that personal relationships with former peers must become less so. Close personal relationships are rarely compatible with effective supervisory ones.

- **Focus early on rites of passage.** The first days are about symbolism more than substance. So focus on rites of passage can help establish you in your new role—for example, having your new boss introduce you to your team and pass the baton.

- **Reenlist your (good) former peers.** For every leader who gets promoted, there are other ambitious souls who wanted the job but didn't get it. So recognize that disappointed competitors will go through stages of adjustment. Focus on figuring out who can work for you and who can't.

- **Establish your authority deftly.** You must walk the knife's edge between over- and underasserting yourself. It can be effective to adopt a consult-and-decide approach when dealing with critical issues until former peers get used to making the calls, as long as you don't make uninformed decisions.

- **Focus on what's good for the business.** From the moment your appointment is announced, some former peers will be straining to discern whether you will play favorites or will seek to advance political agendas at their expense. One antidote is to adopt a relentless, principled focus on doing what is right for the business.

Build Credibility

In your first few weeks in your new job, you cannot hope to have a measurable impact on performance, but you can score small victories and signal that things are changing. Think of this as an effort to secure early, early wins by building your personal credibility.

Your credibility, or lack of it, will depend on how people would answer the following questions about you:

- Do you have the insight and steadiness to make tough decisions?

- Do you have values that they relate to, admire, and want to emulate?

- Do you have the right kind of energy?

- Do you demand high levels of performance from yourself and others?

For better or worse, they will begin to form opinions based on little data. Your early actions, good and bad, will shape perceptions. Once opinion about you has begun to harden, it is difficult to change. And the opinion-forming process happens remarkably quickly.

So how do you build personal credibility? In part, it's about marketing yourself effectively, much akin to building equity in a brand. You want people to associate you with attractive capabilities, attitudes, and values. There's no single right answer for how to do this. In general, though, new leaders are perceived as more credible when they display these characteristics:

- **Demanding but able to be satisfied.** Effective leaders get people to make realistic commitments and then hold them responsible for achieving results. But if you're never satisfied, you'll sap people's motivation. Know when to celebrate success and when to push for more.

- **Accessible but not too familiar.** Being accessible does not mean making yourself available indiscriminately. It means being approachable, but in a way that preserves your authority.

- **Decisive but judicious.** New leaders communicate their capacity to take charge, perhaps by rapidly making some low-consequence decisions, without jumping too quickly into decisions that they aren't ready to make. Early in your transition, you want to project decisiveness but defer some decisions until you know enough to make the right calls.

- **Focused but flexible.** Avoid setting up a vicious cycle and alienating others by coming across as rigid and unwilling to consider multiple solutions. Effective new leaders establish authority by zeroing in on issues but consulting others and encouraging input. They also know when to give people the flexibility to achieve results in their own ways.

- **Active without causing commotion.** There's a fine line between building momentum and overwhelming your group or unit. Make things happen, but avoid pushing people to the point of burnout. Learn to pay attention to stress levels and pace yourself and others.

- **Willing to make tough calls but humane.** You may have to make tough calls right away, including letting go of marginal performers. Effective new leaders do what needs to be done, but they do it in ways that preserve people's dignity and that others perceive as fair. Keep in mind that people watch not only what you do but also how you do it.

Plan to Engage

Because your earliest actions will have a disproportionate influence on how you're perceived, think through how you will get connected to your new organization in the first few days in your new role. What messages do you want to get across about who you are and what you represent as a leader? What are the best ways to convey those messages?

Identify your key audiences—direct reports, other employees, key outside constituencies—and craft a few messages tailored to each. These need not be about what you plan to do; that's premature. They should focus instead on who you are, the values and goals you represent, your style, and how you plan to conduct business.

Think about modes of engagement, too. *How* will you introduce yourself? Should your first meetings with direct reports be one-on-one or in a group? Will these meetings be informal get-to-know-you sessions, or will they immediately focus on business issues and assessment? What other channels, such as e-mail and video, will you use to introduce yourself more widely? Will you have early meetings at other locations where your organization has facilities?

As you make progress in getting connected, identify and act as quickly as you can to remove minor but persistent irritants. Focus on strained external relationships, and begin to repair them. Cut out redundant meetings, shorten excessively long ones, or improve problems with physical work spaces. All this helps you build personal credibility early on.

Finally, keep in mind that effective learning builds personal credibility. It's never a bad thing to be seen as genuinely committed to understanding your new organization. It helps immunize you against the perception that you have come in with your mind made up about the organization's problems and have "the" answer. An early, visible focus on learning signals to the organization that you understand it has a unique history and dynamics. Of course, it's important that you also be seen as a quick study and not, as was said of one president, that you have "a learning curve as flat as Kansas."[4] Know, too, when to shift the emphasis from learning to decision and action.

Write Your Own Story

Your actions during your first few weeks inevitably will have a disproportionate impact, because they are as much about symbolism as about substance. Early actions often get transformed into stories, which can define you as hero or villain. Do you take the time to informally introduce yourself to the support staff, or do you focus only on your boss, peers, and direct reports? Something as simple as this action can help brand you as either accessible or remote. How you introduce yourself to the organization, how you treat support staff, how you deal with small irritants—all these pieces of behavior can become the kernels of stories that circulate widely.

To nudge your mythology in a positive direction, look for and leverage *teachable moments*. These are actions—such as the way Elena dealt with recalcitrant supervisors—that clearly display what you're about; they also model the kinds of behavior you want to encourage. They need not be dramatic statements or confrontations. They can be as simple, and as hard, as asking the penetrating question that crystallizes your group's understanding of a key problem the members are confronting.

Launch Early-Win Projects

Building personal credibility and developing some key relationships help you get immediate wins. Soon, however, you should identify opportunities to get quick, tangible performance improvement in the business. The best candidates are problems you can tackle quickly with modest expenditures and will yield visible operational and financial gains. Examples include bottlenecks that restrict productivity and incentive programs that undermine performance by causing conflict.

Identify three or four key areas, at most, where you will seek to achieve rapid improvement. Use the early wins evaluation tool in table 5-2 to gauge the potential. But keep in mind that if you take on too many initiatives, you risk losing focus. Think about risk management: build a promising portfolio of early-win initiatives

TABLE 5-2

Early wins evaluation tool

This tool helps you assess the potential of candidate focal points for getting early wins. Complete one for each candidate focal point, carefully answering the evaluation questions. Then total the scores for the evaluation question, and use the result as a rough indicator of the potential.

For each of the following questions, circle the response that best describes the potential.

	Not at all	To a small extent	Somewhat	To a signifi- cant extent	To a great extent
Does the focal point offer an opportunity to make a substantial improvement in the performance of your unit?	0	1	2	3	4
Is this improvement achievable in a reasonably short time with available resources?	0	1	2	3	4
Would success also help lay the foundation for achieving agreed-to business goals?	0	1	2	3	4
Will the process used to achieve the win help you make needed changes in behavior in the organization?	0	1	2	3	4

Now total the numbers that you circled, and fill in that number here: _____

The result will be a number between 0 and 16 that is a rough measure you can use to compare the attractiveness of candidate focal points. Use common sense in interpreting these numbers. If the candidate scores 0 on the first question, for example, it doesn't matter if it scores 4's on all the others.

so that big successes in one will balance disappointments in others. Then focus relentlessly on getting results.

To set the stage for securing early wins, make sure your learning agenda specifically addresses how you will identify promising opportunities for improvement. Then translate your goals into specific projects to secure early wins, using the following guidelines:

- **Keep your long-term goals in mind.** Your actions should, to the greatest extent possible, serve your agreed-to business goals and supporting objectives for behavior change.

- **Identify a few promising focal points.** Focal points are areas or processes (such as the customer service processes for Elena) in which improvement can dramatically strengthen the organization's overall operational or financial performance. Concentration on a few focal points will help you reduce the time and energy needed to achieve tangible results. And success in improving performance early in these areas will win you freedom and space to pursue more extensive changes.

- **Launch early-win projects.** Manage your early-win initiatives as projects, targeted at your chosen focal points. This is what Elena did when she appointed a team to improve customer service in her new position.

- **Elevate change agents.** Identify the people in your new unit, at all levels, who have the insight, drive, and incentives to advance your agenda. Promote them or appoint them to lead key projects, as Elena did.

- **Leverage the early-win projects to introduce new behaviors.** Your early-win projects should serve as models of how you want your organization, unit, or group to function in the future. Elena understood this when she engaged a consultant to help the team use the right methods to pursue the project so they could learn how best to do this.

Use the project planning template in table 5-3 to plan projects with maximum impact.

TABLE 5-3

FOGLAMP project checklist

FOGLAMP is an acronym for focus, oversight, goals, leadership, abilities, means, and process. This tool can help you cut through the haze and plan your critical projects. Complete the table for each early-win project you set up.

Project: _____

Question	Answer
Focus: What is the focus for this project? For example, what goal or early win do you want to achieve?	
Oversight: How will you oversee this project? Who else should participate in oversight to help you get buy-in for implementing results?	
Goals: What are the goals and the intermediate milestones and time frames for achieving them?	
Leadership: Who will lead the project? What training, if any, do they need in order to be successful?	
Abilities: What mix of skills and representation needs to be included? Who needs to be included because of their skills? Because they represent key constituencies?	
Means: What additional resources, such as facilitation, does the team need to be successful?	
Process: Are there change models or structured processes you want the team to use? If so, how will they become familiar with the approach?	

Leading Change

As you work out where to get your early wins, think, too, about how you will make change happen in your organization. Keep in mind there is no one best way to lead change; the best approaches depend on the situation. For example, approaches that work well in turnarounds, where there already is a sense of urgency, can fail miserably in realignments, where many people may be in denial about the need for change. So stay open to the possibility that you will lead change differently in different parts of your STARS portfolio.

Planning Versus Learning

Once you've identified the most important problems or issues you need to address, the next step is to decide whether to engage in planned change or collective learning.[5]

The straightforward plan-then-implement approach to change works well when you're sure you have the following key supporting planks in place:

- **Awareness.** A critical mass of people is aware of the need for change.

- **Diagnosis.** You know what needs to be changed and why.

- **Vision.** You have a compelling vision and a solid strategy.

- **Plan.** You have the expertise to put together a detailed plan.

- **Support.** You have sufficiently powerful alliances to support implementation.

This approach often works well in turnaround situations—for example, where people accept there is a problem, the fixes are more technical than cultural or political, and people are hungry for a solution.

If any of these five conditions is not met, however, the pure planning approach to change can get you into trouble. If you're in a realignment, for example, and people are in denial about the need for change, they're likely to greet your plan with stony silence or active resistance. You may therefore need to build awareness of the need for change. Or you may need to sharpen the diagnosis of the problem, create a compelling vision and strategy, develop a solid cross-functional implementation plan, or create a coalition in support of change.

To accomplish any of these goals, you would be well advised to focus on setting up a collective learning process and not on developing and imposing change plans. If many people in the organization are willfully blind to emerging problems, for example, you must put in place a process to pierce this veil. Rather than mount a frontal assault on the organization's defenses, you should engage in something akin to guerrilla warfare, slowly chipping away at people's resistance and raising their awareness of the need for change.

You can do this by exposing key people to new ways of operating and thinking about the business, such as new data on customer satisfaction and competitive offerings. Or you can do some benchmarking of best-in-class organizations, getting the group to analyze how your best competitors perform. Or you can persuade people to envision new approaches to doing things—for example, by scheduling an off-site meeting to brainstorm about key objectives or ways to improve existing processes.

The key, then, is to figure out which parts of the change process can be best addressed through planning, and which are better dealt with through collective learning. Think of a change you want to make in your new organization. Now use the diagnostic flow chart in figure 5-2 to figure out where planning and learning processes are likely to be important to your success.

FIGURE 5-2

Diagnostic framework for managing change

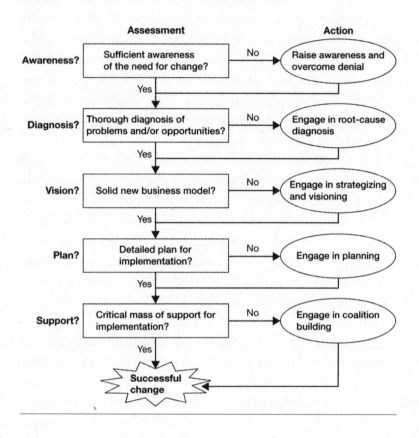

Get Started on Behavior Change

As you plan to get early wins, remember that the means you use are as important as the ends you achieve. The initiatives you put in place to get early wins should do double duty by establishing new standards of behavior. Elena did this when she carefully staffed and coached her project team and then quickly implemented its recommendations.

To change your organization, you will likely have to change its culture. This is a difficult undertaking. Your organization may have well-ingrained bad habits that you want to break. But we know how difficult it is for one person to change habitual patterns in any significant way, never mind a mutually reinforcing collection of people.

Simply blowing up the existing culture and starting over is rarely the right answer. People—and organizations—have limits on the change they can absorb all at once. And organizational cultures invariably have virtues as well as faults; they provide predictability and can be sources of pride. If you send the message that there is nothing good about the existing organization and its culture, you will rob people of a key source of stability in times of change. You also will deprive yourself of a potential wellspring of energy you could tap to improve performance.

The key is to identify both the good and the bad elements of the existing culture. Elevate and praise the good elements even as you seek to change the bad ones. These functional aspects of the familiar culture are a bridge that can help carry people from the past to the future.

Match Strategy to Situation

The choice of behavior-change techniques should be a function of your group's structure, processes, skills, and—above all—situation. Consider again the difference between turnaround and realignment situations. In a turnaround, you face a combination of time pressure and the need to rapidly identify and secure the defensible core of the business. Often, techniques such as bringing in new people from the outside and setting up project teams to pursue specific performance-improvement initiatives are a good fit. Contrast this with realignments, where you are well advised to start with less obvious approaches to behavior change. By changing performance measures and starting benchmarking, for example, you set the stage for collectively creating a vision for realigning the business.

Avoiding Predictable Surprises

Finally, all your efforts to secure early wins could come to naught if you don't pay attention to identifying ticking time bombs and preventing them from exploding in your face. If they do explode, your focus will instantly shift to continuous firefighting, and your hopes for systematically getting established and building momentum will fly out the window.

Some bolts from the blue really do come out of the blue. When this happens, you must grit your teeth and mount the best crisis response you can. But far more often, new leaders are taken off track by predictable surprises. These are situations in which people have all the information necessary to recognize and defuse a time bomb but fail to do so.[6]

This often happens because the new leader simply doesn't look in the right places or ask the right questions. As mentioned earlier, we all have preferences about the types of problems we like to work on and those we prefer to avoid or don't feel competent to address. But you need to discipline yourself either to dig into areas where you're not fully comfortable or to find trustworthy people with the necessary expertise to do so.

Another reason for predictable surprises is that different parts of the organization have different pieces of the puzzle, but no one puts them together. Every organization has its information silos. If you don't put processes in place to make sure critical information is surfaced and integrated, then you're putting yourself at risk of being predictably surprised.

Use the following set of questions to identify areas where potential problems may be lurking:

- **The external environment.** Could trends in public opinion, government action, or economic conditions precipitate major problems for your unit? Examples include a change in government policy that favors competitors or unfavorably influences your prices or costs; a major shift in public opinion about the health or safety implications of using your product; an emerging economic crisis in a developing country.

- **Customers, markets, competitors, and strategy.** Are there developments in the competitive situation confronting your organization that could pose major challenges? Examples include a study suggesting that your product is inferior to that of a competitor; a new competitor that is offering a lower-cost substitute; a price war.

- **Internal capabilities.** Are there potential problems with your unit's processes, skills, and capabilities that could precipitate a crisis? Examples include an unexpected loss of key personnel; major quality problems at a key plant; a product recall.

- **Organizational politics.** Are you in danger of unwittingly stepping on a political land mine? Examples include certain people in your unit who are untouchable, but you don't know it; your failure to recognize that a key peer is subtly undermining you.

As you plan how to secure early wins, keep in mind your overarching goal: creating a virtuous cycle that reinforces wanted behavior and contributes to helping you achieve your agreed-to goals for the organization. Remember that you're aiming at modest but significant early improvements so that you can pursue more fundamental changes.

SECURE EARLY WINS—CHECKLIST

1. Given your agreed-to business goals, what do you need to do during your transition to create momentum for achieving them?

2. How do people need to behave differently to achieve these goals? Describe as vividly as you can the behaviors you need to encourage and those you need to discourage.

3. How do you plan to connect yourself to your new organization? Who are your key audiences, and what messages would you like to convey to them? What are the best modes of engagement?

4. What are the most promising focal points to get some early improvements in performance and start the process of behavior change?

5. What projects do you need to launch, and who will lead them?

6. What predictable surprises could take you off track?

CHAPTER 6

Achieve Alignment

Hannah Jaffey, a respected human resource consultant, was hired by a former client to be corporate vice president of human resources. She joined a company suffering from such intense conflict at the top that some senior executives were barely on speaking terms. Hannah had been brought in to support the CEO in making needed personnel changes and to rebuild the executive team.

Hannah soon realized the organization's structure and incentives system were at the root of the problems. A year earlier, the company, which had grown rapidly, had been reorganized into business units, each focusing on a specific product line. However, several of the units' customer bases overlapped, and the new structure and incentives system discouraged cooperation. The result? Confused customers, conflicts over which units owned key customer relationships, and an inability to offer integrated solutions. The turmoil had begun to impact the financials, with top-line growth stalling and the CEO facing tough questioning from the board and investors.

Convinced the company needed further structural change, Hannah laid out her case to the CEO. But he was reluctant to embark on another round of reorganization, and he remained convinced that the people were the problem. The organizational design was sound, he told Hannah, and with the right people in place it could work.

In truth, there were significant weak links in the executive team. But Hannah knew that the people issues couldn't be dealt with until the structure was put right. So she kept coming back to her boss. She did an in-depth diagnosis and brought to his attention instances in which incentive misalignments had unnecessarily stoked conflict. She also highlighted how other companies had organized themselves to deal with similar tensions.

It took time, but eventually Hannah convinced the CEO to move the company to a hybrid structure. The focus of marketing and sales was returned to customer segments, leaving operations and R&D organized by product line, and a shared-services organization was created to provide finance, HR, IT, and supply chain support. The realignment worked: a year later, the company was functioning much more smoothly, customers were much happier, and robust growth had resumed. And it had become much clearer which executives needed to be replaced.

The higher you climb in organizations, the more you take on the role of *organizational architect*, creating and aligning the key elements of the organizational system: the strategic direction, structure, core processes, and skill bases that provide the foundation for superior performance. No matter how charismatic you are as a leader, you cannot hope to do much if your organization is fundamentally out of alignment. You will feel as if you're pushing a boulder uphill every day.

If you have the scope to alter direction, structure, processes, and skills in your new position, you should begin to analyze the architecture of your organization and assess alignment among these key elements. In the first few months you can't hope to do much more than conduct a solid diagnosis and perhaps get started on the most pressing alignment issues. But it's important to get a handle on what needs to be done so that you can focus some of your early-win projects appropriately and lay the foundation for a subsequent, deeper wave of change.

Even if, like Hannah, you lack the authority to unilaterally alter the architecture of your new organization, you should focus on assessing organizational alignment. Look at how your piece of the puzzle fits (or doesn't fit) into the bigger picture. Think about whether you need to convince influential people—your boss or your peers—that serious misalignments are a key impediment to achieving superior performance. Also, keep in mind that a thorough understanding of organizational systems can help you build credibility with people higher in the organization—and demonstrate your potential for more-senior positions.

Avoiding Common Traps

Many leaders rely on simplistic fixes to address complicated organizational problems, and they end up committing malpractice. Be alert to these common pitfalls:

- **Making changes for change's sake.** The temptation is great for newly appointed leaders to make rapid, visible changes to strategies or structures, whether or not these elements are the right areas for focus. Often, leaders feel self-imposed pressure to put their stamp on the organization and seek to make changes before they really understand the business; it's ready, shoot, aim. Once again, the action imperative creates a sure recipe for disaster.

- **Not adjusting for the STARS situation.** There is no one best way to lead change. The right way to drive organizational alignment in a turnaround (with a focus on rapid and often radical shifts) is very different from the right way to proceed in an accelerated-growth situation or a realignment (when subtle and incremental changes often are the right way to proceed). So it's essential not to adopt a one-size-fits-all approach to change but rather to understand the best ways to proceed in the various STARS situations.

- **Trying to restructure your way out of deeper problems.** Overhauling your organization's structure when the real issues lie in the processes, skill bases, and culture can amount to rearranging the deck chairs on the *Titanic*. Resist doing so until you understand whether restructuring will address the root causes of the problems. Otherwise, you may create new misalignments and have to backtrack, disrupting your organization and damaging your credibility.

- **Creating structures that are too complex.** This is a related trap. It may indeed make sense, as it did in Hannah's situation, to implement a matrix structure. Done well, matrices foster shared accountability and help you work through creative tension. But take care to strike the right balance and not diffuse decision making or introduce sclerotic complexity. Strive, where possible, for clear lines of accountability. Simplify the structure to the greatest degree possible without compromising core goals.

- **Overestimating your organization's capacity to absorb change.** It's easy to envision an ambitious new strategic direction or shift in structure. In practice, though, it can be difficult for people to change in response to large-scale shifts, especially if they have experienced a string of such changes in the recent past. Move quickly if you need to—for example, in a turnaround. But proceed incrementally if the STARS situation permits—for example, in realignments or sustaining-success situations.

Designing Organizational Architecture

Begin by thinking of yourself as the architect of your unit or group. This may be a familiar role for you, but it probably isn't. Few leaders get systematic training in organizational design. Because leaders typically have limited control over organizational design early in their careers, they learn little about it. It's commonplace for less-senior people to complain about obvious misalignments and to wonder why "those idiots" higher up tolerate clearly dysfunctional arrangements. By the time you reach the midsenior levels of most organizations, however, you are well on your way to becoming one of those idiots. You're therefore well advised to begin learning something about how to assess and design organizations.

To design (or redesign) your organization, start by thinking of it as an open system. This is illustrated for an entire business in figure 6-1; you may need to focus on only your piece. The "open" part refers to the reality that organizations are open to (that is, those elements they influence and are influenced by). This reality comprises (1) key players in the external environment, including customers, distributors, suppliers, competitors, governments, NGOs, investors, and the media, and (2) the internal environment: climate, morale, and culture. So leaders' architectural choices must position the organization to respond to, as well as shape, the realities of the external and internal environments.

FIGURE 6-1

Elements of organizational architecture

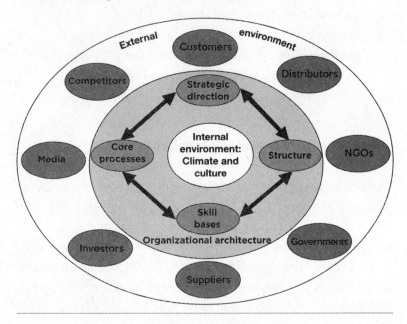

The "systems" part highlights the fact that organizational architectures consist of distinct, interacting elements: strategic direction, structure, core processes, and skill bases. The implication is that you can work on individual elements—for example, change the strategy, alter the structure, streamline a process, or hire people with a different skill set—but you shouldn't do so without thinking through the impact on the other elements. Specifically all four elements of organizational architecture need be aligned to work together.[1]

- **Strategic direction.** The organization's mission, vision, and strategy

- **Structure.** How people are organized in units and how their work is coordinated, measured, and incentivized

- **Core processes.** The systems used to add value through the processing of information and materials

- **Skill bases.** The capabilities of key groups of people in the organization

Of course you need to have the right strategic direction to move forward effectively. But misalignments involving any of the other elements can make even the best strategy useless. Strategic direction drives the other elements *and* is influenced by them: if you decide to change your group's direction, you will probably have to alter its structure, processes, and skills to create a fully aligned architecture.

Diagnosing Misalignments

Organizations can end up misaligned in many ways. Your goal during your first 90 days should be to identify potential misalignments and design a plan for correcting them. Common types of misalignments include the following:

- **Misalignments between strategic direction and skill bases.** Suppose you head an R&D group and your goal is to increase the number of new product ideas your team generates and tests. However, your staff is not up to speed on the latest techniques that would let you run more experiments faster than before. In this case, your group's skills do not support its mission.

- **Misalignments between strategic direction and core processes.** Imagine that you lead a marketing group whose mission is to focus on meeting the needs of a new customer segment. If your team has not established an effective way to compile and analyze information about those customers, your group's systems fail to support the direction. There is a mismatch between strategic direction and core processes.

- **Misalignments between structure and processes.** Suppose you manage a product development group whose members are organized by product line. The rationale for this structure is that it focuses specialized technical expertise on specific products. But this structure has a downside: the group does not have efficient systems for sharing best practices among the various product teams. The resulting mismatch between structure and processes would make it difficult for the entire group to perform optimally.

- **Misalignments between structure and skills.** Suppose the business has recently moved from a functional structure to a matrix structure in an effort to balance product-related and functional decisions. People are used to relying on authority and functional reporting lines to get things done, but now they need to use influence and conflict management skills. The shift in structure has created a mismatch with needed skills that will need to be addressed.

Getting Started

Aligning an organization is like preparing for a long sailing trip. First, you need to be clear on whether your destination (the mission and goals) and your route (the strategy) are the right ones. Then you can figure out which boat you need (the structure), how to outfit it (the processes), and which mix of crew members is best (the skill bases). Throughout the journey, you keep an eye out for reefs that are not on the charts.

The underlying point is that there is a logic to organizational alignment. It's likely to cause problems if you try to change the structure before figuring out whether the direction is the right one. Also, you cannot fully assess the fitness of your existing crew until you have a handle on your destination, route, and boat, although you certainly can get started. Here's how:

1. **Begin with strategic direction.** Take a hard look at how your unit is positioned with respect to the larger organization's goals and your agreed-to priorities. Make sure your mission, vision, and strategy are well thought through and logically integrated.

2. **Look at supporting structure, processes, and skills.** Look at whether your group's existing structure, processes, and skill bases support the strategic direction—either the existing one (if you decide not to change it) or the one you envision. Dig into and understand the relationships among these elements. If one or more of them is ill suited to the mission or strategy you have in mind, figure out how you will either adapt your direction or build (or acquire) the capabilities you need.

3. **Decide how and when you will introduce the new strategic direction.** Armed with a deeper understanding of your group's current capabilities, chart a path for shifting direction (if such a shift is necessary). Sketch out changes in positioning (markets, customers, and suppliers) as well as changes in supporting capabilities. Then adopt a realistic time frame for making these changes.

4. **Think through the correct sequencing.** Different situations demand different approaches to bringing organizations into alignment. In a turnaround, the right

approach often is to alter the strategy (which typically is not adequate), then to bring the structure into alignment with it, and then to focus on supporting processes and skills. In a realignment, however, strategic direction and structure often are not the real source of the difficulties. Instead, they frequently lie in the processes and skill bases of the organization, and these are the places to focus on.

5. **Close the loop.** As you learn more about your group's structure, processes, and skills, you will gain insight into the team's capabilities and its cultural capacity for change. This insight will in turn deepen your understanding of what changes in strategic positioning are possible over what time period.

Defining Strategic Direction

Strategic direction encompasses mission, vision, and strategy. Mission is about *what* will be achieved, vision is about *why* people should feel motivated to perform at a high level, and strategy is about *how* resources should be allocated and decisions made to accomplish the mission. If you keep in mind the what, the why, and the how, you won't get lost in debates about what a mission is, what a vision is, and what a strategy is.

Some fundamental questions about strategic direction concern what the organization will do and, critically, what it will not do. Focus on customers, capital, capabilities, and commitments:

- **Customers.** Which set of existing customers (external or internal) will we continue to serve? What is our value proposition? Which markets are we going to exit? What new markets are we going to enter, and when?

- **Capital.** Of the businesses we will remain in, which will we invest in, and which will we draw cash from? What additional capital is likely to be required, and when? Where will it come from?

- **Capabilities.** What are we good at and not good at? What existing organizational capabilities (for example, a strong new-product development organization) can we leverage? Which do we need to build up? Which do we need to create or acquire?

- **Commitments.** What critical decisions do we need to make about resource commitments? When? What difficult-to-reverse past commitments do we have to live with or try to unwind?

It is beyond the scope of this book to delve deeply into the development of strategic direction, but excellent resources are available to help you answer these questions. Our focus here is on assessing the current direction by looking at its coherence, adequacy, and implementation.

Assess Coherence

Is there a clear logic to the choices that have been made about customers, products, technologies, plans, and resource commitments? To assess whether the elements of strategic direction fit together, you need to look at the logic behind the strategy to ensure that it makes sense overall. Have the people who defined it thought through all its ramifications and the practical aspects of implementing it?

How do you evaluate the logic of the organization's strategic direction? Start by looking at documents that describe your group's mission, vision, and strategy. Then disassemble them into their components: markets, products, technologies, functional plans, and goals. Ask yourself, Do the various dimensions support one another? Is there a logical thread connecting the various parts? To be more specific, is there an obvious connection between market analysis and the group's objectives? Does the product development budget jibe with the capital investments projected in the operations part of the strategy? Are plans in place to train salespeople for new products in the pipeline?

If the organization's strategic direction makes sense overall, you will spot such connections easily.

Assess Adequacy

Is the defined direction sufficient for what your unit needs to do in the next two or three years? Will it be sufficient to support the larger organization's goals? Your group may have a well-thought-through and logically integrated strategic direction. But is it also adequate? That is, will it empower the group to carry out what it needs to do to succeed—and to help the larger organization succeed—in the next two or three years?

To assess adequacy, use these three approaches:

- **Ask probing questions.** Does your boss believe the current direction will provide enough return on the effort your group will expend to implement it? Are there plans in place to secure, develop, and preserve resources for carrying it out? Are profit and other targets high enough to keep the group on the right track? Is enough money earmarked for capital investment? For research?

- **Use a variation on the well-known SWOT method.** See the box "From SWOT to TOWS."

- **Probe the history of how strategic direction got defined.** Find out who drove the process of defining strategic direction. Was it done in a rush? If so, the developers might not have thought through all the ramifications. Did it take a long time? If so, it might represent a lowest-common-denominator compromise that emerged from a political battle. Any mistakes during the development process could compromise the strategy's adequacy.

From SWOT to TOWS

SWOT is arguably the most useful (and certainly the most misunderstood) framework for conducting strategic analysis. The reason has to do with how the tool was developed and, critically, how it was named. SWOT—an acronym for strengths, weaknesses, opportunities, and threats—was originally developed by a team at the Stanford Research Institute (SRI) in the late 1960s.[2] The group came up with the idea of simultaneously analyzing internal capabilities (strengths and weaknesses) and developments in the external environment (threats and opportunities) to identify strategic priorities and develop plans to address them.

Unfortunately, the developers named their method SWOT, with the implication that the analysis should be carried out in that order—first, internal strengths and weaknesses, and then external opportunities and threats. This implied hierarchy has created no end of problems for those who use the methodology to drive strategy discussions in teams. The problem is that in the absence of something to anchor the discussion, an analysis of organizational strengths and weaknesses can very easily become abstract, undirected navel-gazing. As a result, groups often fail in trying to define their organization's strengths and weaknesses, end up frustrated and exhausted, and so give short shrift to critical developments in the external environment.

The correct approach is to start with the environment and then analyze the organization. The first step is to assess the organization's external environment, looking for emerging threats and potential opportunities. Naturally this assessment must be conducted by people who are grounded in the reality of the organization and knowledgeable about its environment.

Having identified potential threats and opportunities, the group should next evaluate them with reference to organizational capabilities. Does the organization have weaknesses that make it particularly vulnerable to specific threats? Does the organization have strengths that would permit it to pursue specific opportunities?

The final step is to translate these assessments into a set of strategic priorities, blunting critical threats and pursuing high-potential opportunities. These are then the inputs to a more extensive strategic planning process.

The confusion that has flowed from naming the method SWOT is so pervasive that a name change is probably in order. The alternative? Call it TOWS, so that people get the right cues about the best order for conducting the process.

Assess Implementation

Have the mission, vision, and strategy of your organization been pursued energetically? If not, why not? Look at how your group's strategic direction is being implemented—what people are *doing* and not what they are saying. This approach will help you pinpoint whether problems stem from inadequacies in *formulation* or *implementation*. Ask yourself these kinds of questions:

- Is our overall pattern of decisions consistent with our defined direction? What goals does the organization actually seem to be pursuing?

- Are we using the specified performance metrics to make day-to-day decisions?

- If implementation requires teamwork and cross-functional integration, are people acting as teams and collaborating across functions?

- If implementation requires the development of new employee skills, is a learning-and-development infrastructure in place to develop those skills?

Your answers to these kinds of questions will tell you whether to push for changes in your group's strategic direction or in its implementation.

Modify Strategic Direction

Suppose you discover serious flaws in the mission, vision, and strategy you have inherited. Can you radically change them or the way they're implemented? That depends on two factors: the STARS situation you're entering, and your ability to persuade others and build support for your ideas.

If you believe that your group is on the wrong path, you need to raise questions to persuade your boss and others to reexamine strategic direction. If you conclude that the existing strategy will move the group forward, but neither fast enough nor far enough, the wisest course may be to tweak it early on and plan for bigger changes later. For example, you might raise the targeted revenue goals modestly or recommend investing in a needed technology sooner than the strategic direction calls for. More fundamental changes should wait until you've learned more and have built support among key constituencies.

Shaping Your Group's Structure

Whether or not you decide to change the strategic direction of your organization, you still need to assess the adequacy of the structure. If the structure doesn't support the strategy—either the existing one or a new one you plan to put in place—your organization's energies will not be directed appropriately.

One caution: much of an organization's power gets allocated via its structure, because it defines who has the authority to do what. So take care not to take on structural change unless it is obvious that it's needed—for example, in turnaround or rapid-growth scenarios. Tackling structural change early on can be particularly perilous in realignments, where there isn't a burning platform to drive the change process.

What is structure exactly? Most simply, your group's structure is the way it organizes people and technology to support the mission, vision, and strategy. Structure consists of the following elements:

- **Units:** How your direct reports are grouped, such as by function, product, or geographical area

- **Reporting relationships and integration mechanisms:** How lines of reporting and accountability are set up to coordinate effort, and how work among units is integrated

- **Decision rights and rules:** Who is empowered to make what kinds of decisions, and what rules should be applied to align decisions with strategy

- **Performance measurement and incentive systems:** The performance-evaluation metrics and incentive systems that are in place

Assess Structure

Before you begin to generate ideas for reshaping your group's structure, look into the interaction of the four structural elements. Are the pieces out of tune or in harmony? Ask yourself these questions:

- Does the grouping of team members help us achieve our mission and implement the strategy? Are the right people in the right places to work toward our core objectives?

- Do reporting relationships help align effort? Is it clear who is accountable for what? Is the work of different units integrated effectively?

- Is the allocation of decision rights helping us make the best decisions to support the strategy? Is the right balance achieved between centralization and decentralization? Between standardization and customization?

- Are we measuring and rewarding the kinds of achievements that matter most to our strategic aims? Is the balance right between fixed rewards and performance-based rewards? Between individual incentives and group incentives?

If you're in a start-up situation—and therefore forming a new group—you will not have existing structures to evaluate. Instead, think about how you want the structural pieces to work in your group.

Grapple with the Trade-Offs

There is no perfect organizational structure; every one embodies trade-offs. Thus, your challenge is to find the right balance for your situation. As you consider changes in your group's structure, keep in mind some common problems that can arise:

- **The organization has silos of excellence.** When you group people with similar experience and capabilities, they can accumulate deep wells of expertise. But they can also become isolated and compartmentalized. The implication is that you need to pay attention to how integration happens. This includes looking at who is responsible for bridging the chasms between functions, as well as identifying whether the right integration mechanisms, such as cross-functional teams and group performance incentives, are in place.

- **Employees' decision-making scope is too narrow or too broad.** A good general rule is that decisions should be made by the people who have the most relevant knowledge, as long as their incentives encourage them to do what is best for the organization. If your group's decision-making process is centralized, you (and perhaps several other individuals) can decide quickly. But you may be forgoing the benefit of the wisdom of others who have better information to make certain of those decisions. This structure can lead to ill-informed decisions and can tax those who make all the decisions. If, on the other hand, people are given decision-making scope but do not understand the larger implications of their choices, they may make unwise calls.

- **Employees have incentives to do the wrong things.** The best predictor of what people will do is what they are incentivized to do. Effective leaders seek to align the interests of individual decision makers with the interests of the group as a whole. This is why placing more emphasis on group incentives is effective in some organizations: they focus everyone's attention on the ability to work together. Problems arise when measurement and compensation schemes fail to reward employees for either their individual *or* their collective efforts. Problems also arise when rewards advance employees' individual interests at the expense of the group's broader goals—for example, when multiple employees who could serve the same set of customers lack incentives to cooperate. This was the problem confronting Hannah in the story at the beginning of the chapter.

- **Reporting relationships lead to compartmentalization or diffusion of accountability.** Reporting relationships help you observe and control the workings of your group, clarify responsibility, and encourage accountability. Hierarchical reporting relationships make these tasks easier but can lead to compartmentalization and poor information sharing. Complex reporting arrangements, such as matrix structures, broaden information sharing and reduce compartmentalization but can diffuse accountability.

Aligning Core Processes

Core processes (often referred to as "systems") enable your group to transform information, materials, and knowledge into value in the form of commercially viable products or services, new knowledge or ideas, productive relationships, or anything else the larger organization considers essential. Again, as with structure, ask yourself whether the processes currently in place support your mission, vision, and strategy.

Make the Right Trade-Offs

Keep in mind that the extent and types of processes you need depend on the trade-offs you need to make. Think, for example, about whether your primary goal is to drive flawless execution or to stimulate innovation.[3] You can't hope to execute with high levels of quality and reliability (and low costs) without an intensive focus on developing processes that specify both the ends and the means (methods, techniques, tools) in exquisite detail. Obvious examples are manufacturing plants and service delivery organizations. But these same sorts of processes can impede innovation. So if stimulating innovation is your goal, you may need to develop processes that focus on defining ends and rigorously checking progress toward achieving them at key milestones, and not so much on controlling the means people use to achieve the results.

Analyze Processes

A credit card company that sought to identify its core processes came up with the results shown in table 6-1. It then mapped and improved each of these processes, developing appropriate measurement schemes and altering reward systems to better align behaviors. It also focused on identifying key bottlenecks. For critical tasks that were insufficiently under control, the company revamped procedures and introduced new support tools. The result was a dramatic increase in both customer satisfaction and the productivity of the organization.

Your unit or group may have just as many processes as the credit card company. Your first challenge is to identify those

TABLE 6-1

Process analysis example

Production/Service-delivery processes	Support/Service processes	Business processes
Application processing	Collections	Quality management
Credit screening	Customer inquiry	Financial management
Credit card production	Relationship management	Human resource management
Authorizations management	Information and technology management	
Transaction processing		
Billing		
Payment processing		

processes and then to decide which of them are most important to your strategy. For example, suppose your group's strategy emphasizes customer satisfaction over product development. You would want to ensure that all the processes involved in delivery of products or services to customers support that goal.

Align Processes with Structure

If your group's core processes are to support its strategic direction, they must also align with the unit's structure (the way people and work are organized). We can compare this relationship to the human body. Our anatomy—skeleton, musculature, skin, and other components—is the structural foundation for the body's normal functions. Our physiology—circulation, respiration, digestion, and so on—is the set of systems (or processes) that enable the various parts of the body to work together. In organizations, as in human bodies, both the structure and the processes must be sound and must reinforce one another.

To evaluate the efficiency and effectiveness of each core process, you should examine four aspects:

- **Productivity.** Does the process efficiently transform knowledge, materials, and labor into value?

- **Timeliness.** Does the process deliver the desired value in a timely manner?

- **Reliability.** Is the process sufficiently reliable, or does it break down too often?

- **Quality.** Does the process deliver value in a way that consistently meets required quality standards?

When processes and structure mesh with each other, the good results are clear to see. For example, a customer service organization structured around specific customer segments also shares information across teams and responds effectively to issues that affect all customer groups.

But when processes and structure are at odds—as when different teams compete for the same set of customers using different sales processes—they hamstring one another and subvert the group's strategy.

Improve Core Processes

How do you actually improve a core process? Start by making a *process* (or *work-flow*) *map*—a straightforward diagram of exactly how the tasks in a particular process flow through the individuals and groups who handle them. Figure 6-2 shows a simplified process map for order fulfillment.

Ask the individuals responsible for each stage of the process to chart the process flow from beginning to end. Then ask the team

FIGURE 6-2

A process map

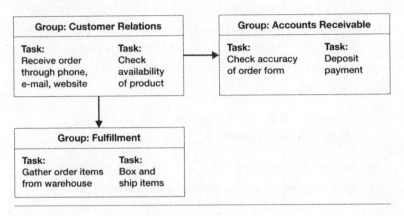

to look for bottlenecks and problem interfaces between individuals responsible for adjacent sets of tasks. For example, errors or delays may occur when someone in customer relations communicates to the fulfillment group the need for special handling of an order. Process failures are commonplace during hand-offs of this kind. Work with the team to identify opportunities for high-leverage improvements.

Process analysis stimulates collective learning. It helps the entire group understand exactly who does what, within and between units or groups, to carry out a particular process. Creating a process or work-flow map also sheds light on how problems arise. You, your boss, and your group can then decide how best to improve the process—for example, by streamlining and automating work flows.

A few words of caution. You are probably responsible for a number of processes. If so, manage them as a portfolio, focusing on a few at a time. Take care to factor in your organization's capacity to absorb change.

Developing Your Group's Skill Bases

Do your direct reports have the skills and knowledge they need to perform your group's core processes superbly—and thus to support the strategy you have identified? If not, the entire architecture of your group could be compromised. A skill base comprises these four types of knowledge:

- **Individual expertise.** Gained through training, education, and experience

- **Relational knowledge.** An understanding of how to work together to integrate individual knowledge to achieve specified goals

- **Embedded knowledge.** The core technologies on which your group's performance depends, such as customer databases or R&D technologies

- **Metaknowledge.** The awareness of where to go to get critical information—for example, through external affiliations such as research institutions and technology partners

Identify Gaps and Resources

The overarching goal of assessing your group's capabilities is to identify (1) critical gaps between needed and existing skills and knowledge and (2) underutilized resources, such as partially exploited technologies and squandered expertise. Closing gaps and making better use of underutilized resources can produce significant gains in performance and productivity.

To identify skill and knowledge gaps, first revisit your mission and strategy and the core processes you identified. Ask yourself what mix of the four types of knowledge is needed to support your group's core processes. Treat this as a visioning exercise in which you imagine the ideal knowledge mix. Then assess your group's existing skills, knowledge, and technologies. What gaps do you see? Which of them can be repaired quickly, and which will take more time?

To identify underutilized resources, search for individuals or groups in your unit who have performed much better than average. What has enabled them to do so? Do they enjoy resources (technologies, methods, materials, and support from key people) that could be exported to the rest of your unit? Have promising product ideas been sitting on the shelf because of lack of interest or investment? Could existing production resources be adapted to serve new sets of customers?

Changing Architecture to Change Culture

Keep in mind that culture is not something you can change directly. It is powerfully influenced by the four elements of organizational architecture, as well as by leadership behaviors. The implication is that to change the culture, you need to change the architecture as well as reinforce what you're trying to do with the right leadership.

One example is changing the metrics by which you judge success and then aligning employees' objectives and incentives with those new measures. For instance, consider changing the balance between individual and group incentives. Does success require people to work closely and coordinate with one another—for example, in a new-product development team? If so, then put more weight on group incentives. Do people in your group operate independently—for example, in a sales unit? If so, and if their individual contributions to the business can be measured, then place more emphasis on individual incentives.

Getting Aligned

Draw on all the analyses discussed in this chapter to develop a plan for aligning your organization. If you're repeatedly frustrated in your efforts to get people to adopt more productive behaviors, step back and ask whether organizational misalignments might be creating problems.

ACHIEVE ALIGNMENT—CHECKLIST

1. What are your observations about misalignments among strategic direction, structure, processes, and skills? How will you dig deeper to confirm or refine your impressions?

2. What decisions about customers, capital, capabilities, and commitments do you need to make? How and when will you make these decisions?

3. What is your current assessment of the coherence of the organization's strategic direction? Of its adequacy? What are your current thoughts about changing direction?

4. What are the strengths and weaknesses of the organization's structure? What potential structural changes are you thinking about?

5. What are the core processes in your organization? How well are they performing? What are your priorities for process improvement?

6. What skill gaps and underutilized resources have you identified? What are your priorities for strengthening key skill bases?

CHAPTER 7

Build Your Team

When Liam Geffen was appointed to lead a troubled business unit of a process automation company, he knew he was in for an uphill climb. The extent of the challenge became clearer when he read the previous year's performance evaluations for his new team. Everyone was either outstanding or marginal; there was nobody in between. It seemed his predecessor had played favorites.

Conversations with his new direct reports and a thorough review of operating results confirmed Liam's suspicion that the performance evaluations were skewed. In particular, the VP of marketing seemed reasonably competent but by no means a minor god. Unfortunately, he believed his own press. The VP of sales struck Liam as a solid performer who had been scapegoated for poor judgment calls by Liam's predecessor. The relationship between marketing and sales was understandably tense.

Liam recognized that one or both of the VPs would probably have to go. He met with each of them separately and bluntly told them how he viewed their performance ratings. He then laid out detailed two-month plans for each. Meanwhile, he and his VP for human resources quietly launched outside searches for both positions. Liam also held skip-level meetings with midlevel people to assess the depth of talent and to look for promising candidates for the top jobs.

By the end of his third month, Liam had signaled to the marketing VP that he would not make it; he soon left and was replaced by one of his direct reports. Meanwhile, the head of sales had risen to Liam's challenge. Now Liam was confident he had strong performers in these two key positions and was ready to move forward.

Liam recognized that he couldn't afford to have the wrong people on his team. If, like most new leaders, you inherit a group of direct reports, it is essential to build your team to marshal the talent you need to achieve superior results. The most important decisions you make in your first 90 days will probably be about people. If you succeed in creating a high-performance team, you can exert tremendous leverage in value creation. If not, you will face severe difficulties, for no leader can hope to achieve much alone. Bad early personnel choices will almost certainly haunt you.

But even though finding the right people is essential, it is not enough. Begin by assessing existing team members (direct and indirect reports) to decide what changes you need to make. Then devise a plan for getting new people and moving the people you retain into the right positions—without doing too much damage to short-term performance in the process. Even this is not enough. You still need to align and motivate your team members to propel them in desired directions. Finally, you must establish new processes to promote teamwork.

Avoiding Common Traps

Many new leaders stumble when it comes to building their teams. The result may be a significant delay in reaching the break-even point, or it may be outright derailment. These are some of the characteristic traps into which you can fall:

- **Criticizing the previous leadership.** There is nothing to be gained by criticizing the people who led the organization before you arrived. This doesn't mean that you need to condone poor past performance, nor does it mean that you can't highlight problems. Of course you need to evaluate the impact of previous leadership, but rather than point out others' mistakes, concentrate on assessing current behavior and results and on making the changes necessary to support improved performance.

- **Keeping the existing team too long.** Unless you are in a start-up, you do not get to build a team from scratch; you inherit a team and must mold it into what you need to achieve your A-item priorities. Some leaders make major changes in their teams too precipitously, but it is more common to keep people longer than is wise. Whether because they're afflicted with hubris ("These people have not performed well because they lacked a leader like me") or because they shy away from tough personnel calls, leaders end up with less-than-outstanding teams. This means they and the other strong performers must shoulder more of the load themselves. The extent of team change and the time frame for making shifts depends on the STARS situation you confront; it may be shorter in a turnaround, and longer in a realignment situation. Also, there may be constraints on your ability to make changes; you may have to accept that and figure out how to get the most out of the people you've inherited—for example, by defining roles. In any case, you should establish deadlines for reaching conclusions about your team and taking action within your 90-day plan, and then stick to them.

- **Not balancing stability and change.** Building a team you've inherited is like repairing a leaky ship in mid-ocean. You will not reach your destination if you ignore the necessary repairs, but you do not want to try to change too much too fast and sink the ship. The key is to find the right balance between stability and change. First and foremost, focus only on truly high-priority personnel changes early on. If you can make do for a while with a B-player, then do so.

- **Not working on organizational alignment and team development in parallel.** A ship's captain cannot make the right choices about his crew without knowing the destination, the route, and the ship. Likewise, you can't build your team in isolation from changes in strategic direction, structure, processes, and skill bases. Otherwise, you could end up with the right people in the wrong jobs. As figure 7-1 illustrates, your efforts to assess the organization and achieve alignment should go on in parallel with assessment of the team and necessary personnel changes.

- **Not holding on to the good people.** One experienced manager shared hard-won lessons about the dangers of losing good people. "When you shake the tree," she said, "good people can fall out, too." Her point is that uncertainty about who will and will not be on the team can lead your best people to move elsewhere. Although there are constraints on what you can say about who will stay and who will go, you should look for ways to signal to the top performers that you recognize their capabilities. A little reassurance goes a long way.

- **Undertaking team building before the core is in place.** It is tempting to launch team-building activities right away, but this approach poses a danger; it strengthens bonds in a group, some of whose members may be leaving. So avoid explicit team-building activities until the team you want is largely in place. This does not mean, of course, that you should avoid meeting as a group. Just keep the focus on the business.

- **Making implementation-dependent decisions too early.** When successful implementation of key initiatives requires buy-in from your team, you should judiciously defer making decisions until the core members are in place. Of course there will be decisions you cannot afford to delay, but it can be counterproductive to make decisions that commit new people to courses of action they had no part in defining. Carefully weigh the benefits of moving quickly on major initiatives against the lost opportunity of gaining buy-in from the people you will bring on board later.

- **Trying to do it all yourself.** Finally, keep in mind that restructuring a team is fraught with emotional, legal, and company policy complications. Do not try to undertake this on your own. Find out who can best advise you and help you chart a strategy. The support of a good HR person is indispensable to any effort to restructure a team.

FIGURE 7-1

Synchronizing architectural alignment and team restructuring

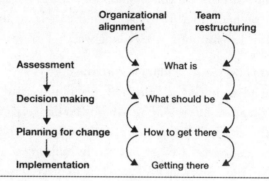

Assuming you avoid these traps, what do you need to do to build your team? Start by rigorously assessing the people you inherited, and then plan to evolve the team into what you need it to be. In parallel with this, work to align the team with your strategic direction and early-win priorities, and put in place the performance-management and decision-making processes you need to lead effectively.

Assessing Your Team

You likely will inherit some outstanding performers (A-players), some average ones (B-players), and some who are simply not up to the job (C-players). You will also inherit a group with its own internal dynamics and politics; some members may even have hoped for your job. During your first 30 to 60 days (depending on the STARS mix you inherited), you need to sort out who's who, what roles people have played, and how the group has worked in the past.

Establish Your Evaluative Criteria

You will inevitably find yourself forming impressions of team members as you meet them and digest results and performance reviews. Don't suppress these early reactions, but be sure to step back from them and undertake a more rigorous evaluation.

The starting point is to be conscious of the criteria you will explicitly or implicitly use to evaluate people who report to you. Consider these six criteria:

- **Competence.** Does this person have the technical competence and experience to do the job effectively?

- **Judgment.** Does this person exercise good judgment, especially under pressure or when faced with making sacrifices for the greater good?

- **Energy.** Does this team member bring the right kind of energy to the job, or is she burned out or disengaged?

- **Focus.** Is this person capable of setting priorities and sticking to them, or prone to riding off in all directions?

- **Relationships.** Does this individual get along with others on the team and support collective decision making, or is he difficult to work with?

- **Trust.** Can you trust this person to keep her word and follow through on commitments?

To get a quick read on the criteria you use, fill out table 7-1. Divide 100 points among the six criteria according to the relative weight you place on them when you evaluate direct reports. Record those numbers in the middle column, making sure they add up to 100. Now identify one of these criteria as your *threshold issue*, meaning that if a person does not meet a basic threshold

TABLE 7-1

Assessment of evaluative criteria

Evaluative criteria	Relative weights (Divide 100 points among the six issues)	Threshold issue (Designate with an asterisk)
Competence		
Judgment		
Energy		
Focus		
Relationships		
Trust		

on that dimension, nothing else matters. Label your threshold issue with an asterisk in the right-hand column.

Now step back. Does this analysis accurately represent the values you apply when you evaluate people on your team? If so, does it suggest any potential blind spots in the way you evaluate people? It is worthwhile to spend some time thinking about the criteria you will use. Having done so, you will be better prepared to make a rigorous and systematic evaluation.

Check Your Assumptions

Your assessments are likely to reflect assumptions you hold about what you can and can't change in the people who work for you. If you score relationships low and judgment high, for example, you may think that relationships within your team are something you can influence, whereas you cannot influence judgment. Likewise, you may have designated trust as a threshold issue—many leaders do—because you believe you must be able to trust those who work for you and because you think trustworthiness is a trait that cannot be changed. You may be right in these assumptions, but it's essential that you be conscious you are making them.

Factor In Functional Expertise

If you're managing a team whose members have diverse functional expertise—such as marketing, finance, operations, and R&D—you need to get a handle on their competence in their respective areas. This task can be daunting, especially for first-time enterprise leaders. If you're an insider, try to solicit the opinions of people you respect in each function who know the individuals on your team. (For more on the transition to enterprise leadership and its challenges, see Michael Watkins, "How Managers Become Leaders," *Harvard Business Review*, June 2012.)

If you're entering an enterprise leader role, consider developing your own templates for evaluating people in functions such as marketing, sales, finance, and operations. A good template includes function-specific key performance indicators (KPIs), what the KPIs should and should not show, key questions to ask, and warning signs. To develop each template, talk to experienced enterprise leaders about what they look for in these functions.

Factor In the Extent of Teamwork

The weights you apply in evaluation should vary depending on the work your direct reports are doing. Suppose, for example, that you're taking a new job as vice president of sales, managing a geographically scattered group of regional sales managers. How would your criteria for evaluating this group differ from those you would apply if you had been named to lead a new-product development project?

These jobs differ sharply in the extent to which your direct reports operate independently. If your direct reports operate more or less independently, their capacity to work together will be far less important than if you were managing an interdependent product development team. In situations like this, it may be perfectly acceptable to have a high-performing group rather than a true team.

Factor In the STARS Mix

The criteria you apply may also depend on your STARS portfolio—the mix of start-up, turnaround, accelerated-growth, realignment, or sustaining-success situations you have inherited. In a sustaining-success situation, for example, you may have the time to develop one or two high-potential members of your team. It may be OK if they currently are B-players, if you are confident you can get them to the A-player level.[1] In a turnaround, by contrast, you need people who can perform at the A-player level right away.

You also should evaluate people based on their STARS experience and capabilities as well as their match to the situation at hand. Suppose, for example, you're taking over a business that was once very successful, started to slide, and wasn't successfully realigned. Now you've been brought in to turn it around. You may have inherited people who would be A-performers in sustaining-success or realignment situations but who are not the types of leaders you need in a turnaround.

Factor In the Criticality of Positions

Finally, your evaluations of team members should depend on how critical their positions are. As you make your assessments, keep in mind it's not only about players but also about positions.[2]

So take some time to assess how important the various positions held by your direct and indirect reports are to your success. If it helps, list the positions and assess the criticality of each on a 1–10 scale. Then keep these assessments in mind as you evaluate the people you inherited.

It's important to do this, because it takes a lot of energy to make changes on your team. It may be all right if you find that you have a B-player in a position that isn't high on the critical list, but not at all acceptable if the position is critical.

Assess Your People

When you begin to assess each team member using the criteria and assessments of position criticality you have developed, the first test is whether any of them fail to meet your threshold requirements. If so, begin planning to replace them. However, merely surviving the basic hurdle does not mean they are keepers. Go on to the next step: evaluate their strengths and weaknesses, factoring in the relative value you assign to each criterion. Now who makes the grade, and who does not?

Meet one-on-one with each member of your new team as soon as possible. Depending on your style, these early meetings might take the form of informal discussions, formal reviews, or a combination, but your own preparation and focus should be standardized:

1. **Prepare for each meeting.** Review available personnel history, performance data, and other appraisals. Familiarize yourself with each person's technical or professional skills so that you can assess how he functions on the team.

2. **Create an interview template.** Ask people the same set of questions, and see how their answers vary. Here are sample questions.

– What are the strengths and weaknesses of our existing strategy?

– What are the biggest challenges and opportunities facing us in the short term? In the medium term?

– What resources could we leverage more effectively?

– How could we improve the way the team works together?

– If you were in my position, what would your priorities be?

3. **Look for verbal and nonverbal clues.** Note choices of words, body language, and hot buttons.

– Notice what the individual does not say. Does the person volunteer information, or do you have to extract it? Does the person take responsibility for problems in her area? Make excuses? Subtly point fingers at others?

– How consistent are the individual's facial expressions and body language with his words?

– What topics elicit strong emotional responses? These hot buttons provide clues to what motivates the individual and what kinds of changes she would be energized by.

– Outside these one-on-one meetings, notice how the individual relates to other team members. Do relations appear cordial and productive? Tense and competitive? Judgmental or reserved?

Test Their Judgment

Make sure you are assessing judgment and not only technical competence or basic intelligence. Some very bright people have lousy business judgment, and some people of average competence have extraordinary judgment. It is essential to be clear about the mix of knowledge and judgment you need from key people.

One way to assess judgment is to work with a person for an extended time and observe whether he is able to (1) make sound predictions and (2) develop good strategies for avoiding problems. Both abilities draw on an individual's *mental models*, or ways of identifying the essential features and dynamics of emerging situations and translating those insights into effective action. This is what expert judgment is all about. The problem, of course, is that you don't have much time, and it can take a while to find out whether someone did or did not make good predictions. Fortunately, there are ways you can accelerate this process.

One way is to test people's judgment in a domain in which feedback on their predictions will emerge quickly. Experiment with the following approach. Ask individuals about a topic they're passionate about outside work. It could be politics or cooking or baseball; it doesn't matter. Challenge them to make predictions: "Who do you think is going to do better in the debate?" "What does it take to bake a perfect soufflé?" "Which team will win the game tonight?" Press them to commit themselves; unwillingness to go out on a limb is a warning sign in itself. Then probe why they think their predictions are correct. Does the rationale make sense? If possible, follow up to see what happens.

What you're testing is a person's capacity to exercise expert judgment in a particular domain. Someone who has become an expert in a private domain is likely to have done so in her chosen field of business, too, given enough passion about it. However you do it, the key is to find ways, beyond just waiting to see how people perform on the job, to probe for the hallmarks of expertise.

Assess the Team as a Whole

In addition to evaluating individual team members, assess how the entire group works. Use these techniques for spotting problems in the team's overall dynamics:

- **Study the data.** Read reports and minutes of team meetings. If your organization conducts climate or morale surveys of individual units, examine these as well.

- **Systematically ask questions.** Assess the individual responses to the common set of questions you asked when you met with individual team members. Are their answers overly consistent? If so, this may suggest an agreed-on party line, but it could also mean that everyone genuinely shares the same impressions of what's going on. It will be up to you to evaluate what you observe. Do the responses show little consistency? If so, the team may lack coherence.

- **Probe group dynamics.** Observe how the team interacts in your early meetings. Do you detect any alliances? Particular attitudes? Leadership roles? Who defers to whom on a given topic? When one person is speaking, do others roll their eyes or otherwise express disagreement or frustration? Pay attention to these signs to test your early insights and detect coalitions and conflicts.

Evolving Your Team

Once you've evaluated individual team members' capabilities, factoring in functional expertise, teamwork requirements, the STARS portfolio, and the criticality of positions, the next step is to figure out how best to deal with each person. By the end of roughly the first 30 days, you should be able to provisionally assign people to one of the following categories:

- **Keep in place.** The person is performing well in her current job.

- **Keep and develop.** The individual needs development, and you have the time and energy to do it.

- **Move to another position.** The person is a strong performer but is not in a position that makes the most of his skills or personal qualities.

- **Replace (low priority).** The person should be replaced, but the situation is not urgent.

- **Replace (high priority).** The person should be replaced as soon as possible.

- **Observe for a while.** This person is still a question mark, and you need to learn more before you can make a definitive judgment about them.

These assessments need not be absolutely irreversible, but you should feel 90-plus percent confident in them. If you remain uncertain about someone, leave her in the "observe" category. As time goes on and you learn more, you can revise and refine your assessments.

Consider Alternatives

You may be tempted to begin right away to act on high-priority replacement decisions. But take a moment first to consider alternatives. Letting an employee go can be difficult and time-consuming. Even if poor performance is well documented, the termination process can take months or longer. If there is no paper trail regarding poor performance, it will take time to document.

In addition, your ability to replace someone at all may depend on a host of factors, including legal protections, cultural norms, and political alliances. Sometimes it simply is not possible to replace someone, even if he is performing miserably. If this is the case, you must figure out how to play the hand you were dealt as well as possible.

Fortunately, you have alternatives. Often, a poor performer will decide to move on of her own accord in response to a clear message from you. Alternatively, you can work with human resources to shift the person to a more suitable position:

- **Shift her role.** Move her to a position on the team that better suits her skills. This is unlikely to be a permanent solution for a problem performer, but it can help you work through the short-term problem of keeping the organization running while you look for the right person to fill the slot.

- **Move her out of the way.** If she simply can't contribute productively or is a disruptive or dispiriting influence, then it is better to have her doing nothing than destroying value. Consider shrinking her responsibilities significantly. This also has the virtue of sending a strong signal to her about your view of her contributions, which may help her see that it would be best to move on.

- **Move her elsewhere in the organization.** Help the person find a suitable position in the larger organization. Sometimes, if handled well, this move can benefit you, the individual, and the organization overall, but don't pursue this solution unless you are genuinely convinced the person can perform well in the new situation. Simply shifting a problem performer onto someone else's shoulders will damage your reputation.

Develop Backups

To keep your team functioning while you build the best possible long-term configuration, you may need to keep an underperformer on the job while searching for a replacement. As soon as you are reasonably sure that someone is not going to make it, begin looking discreetly for a successor. Evaluate other people on your team and elsewhere in the organization for the potential to move up. Use skip-level meetings and regular reporting sessions to evaluate the talent pool. Ask human resources to launch a search.

Treat People Respectfully

During every phase of the team-evolution process, take pains to treat *everyone* with respect. Even if people in your unit agree that a particular person should be replaced, your reputation will suffer if they view your actions as unfair. Do what you can to show people the care with which you are assessing team members' capabilities and the fit between jobs and individuals. Your direct reports will form lasting impressions of you based on how you manage this part of your job.

Aligning Your Team

Having the right people on the team is essential, but it's not enough. To achieve your agreed-to priorities and secure early wins, you need to define how each team member can best support those key goals. This process calls for breaking down large goals into their components and working with your team to assign responsibility for each element. Then it calls for making each individual accountable for managing his goals. How do you encourage accountability?

As illustrated in figure 7-2, a blend of push and pull tools works best to align and motivate a team. *Push tools*, such as goals, performance measurement systems, and incentives, motivate people through authority, loyalty, fear, and expectation of reward for productive work. *Pull tools*, such as a compelling vision, inspire people by invoking a positive and exciting image of the future.

The mix of push and pull you use will depend on your assessment of how people on your team prefer to be motivated. Your high-energy go-getters may respond more enthusiastically to pull incentives. With more methodical and risk-averse folks, push tools may prove more effective.

The right mix also will depend on the STARS situations you're dealing with. Turnarounds typically provide plenty of push. The problem teaches people that something needs to be done. In

FIGURE 7-2

Using push and pull tools to motivate people

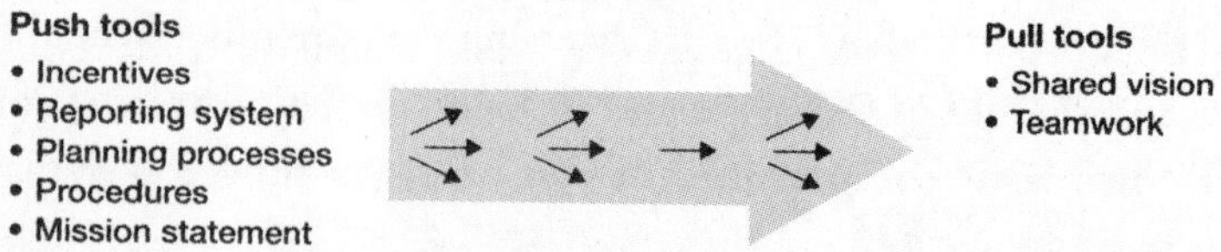

Push tools
- Incentives
- Reporting system
- Planning processes
- Procedures
- Mission statement

Pull tools
- Shared vision
- Teamwork

realignment situations, however, it may be challenging to create a sense of urgency. When this is the case, focus more attention on the pull side of the equation—for example, by defining a compelling vision for what the organization could become.

Define Goals and Performance Metrics

On the push side, establishing—and sticking to—clear and explicit performance metrics is the best way to encourage accountability. Select performance measures that will let you know as clearly as possible whether a team member has achieved her goals.

Avoid ambiguously defined goals, such as "Improve sales" or "Decrease product development time." Instead, define goals in terms that can be quantified. Examples include "Increase sales of product X by 15 to 30 percent over the fourth quarter of this year," or "Decrease development time on product line Y from twelve months to six months within the next two years."

Align Incentives

A baseline question to ask yourself is how best to incentivize team members to achieve desired goals. What mix of monetary and nonmonetary rewards will you employ?

It is equally important to decide whether to base rewards more on individual or collective performance. This decision is linked to your assessment of whether you need true teamwork. If so, put more emphasis on collective rewards. If it is sufficient to have a high-performing group, then place more emphasis on individual performance.

It's important to strike the right balance. If your direct reports work essentially independently and if the group's success hinges chiefly on individual achievement, you don't need to promote teamwork and should consider an individual incentive system. If success depends largely on cooperation among your direct reports and integration of their expertise, true teamwork is essential, and you should use group goals and incentives to gain alignment.

Usually, you will want to create incentives for both individual excellence (when your direct reports undertake independent tasks) and for team excellence (when they undertake interdependent tasks). The correct mix depends on the relative importance of independent and interdependent activity for the overall success of your unit. (See box, "The Incentive Equation.")

The Incentive Equation

The *incentive equation* defines the mix of incentives that you will use to motivate desired performance. Here are the basic formulas:

Total reward = nonmonetary reward + monetary reward

The relative sizes of nonmonetary and monetary rewards depend on (1) the availability of nonmonetary rewards such as advancement and recognition and (2) their perceived importance to the people involved.

Monetary reward = fixed compensation + performance-based compensation

The relative sizes of fixed and performance-based compensation depend on (1) the extent of observability and measurability of people's contributions and (2) the time lag between performance and results. The lower the observability or measurability of contributions and the longer the time lag, the more you should rely on fixed compensation.

Performance-based compensation = individual performance-based compensation + group performance-based compensation

The relative sizes of individual and group-based performance compensation depend on the extent of interdependence of contributions. If superior performance comes from the sum of independent efforts, then individual performance should be rewarded (for example, in a sales group). If group cooperation and integration are critical, then group-based incentives should get more weight (for example, in a new-product development team). Note that there may be several levels of group-based incentives: team, unit, and company as a whole.

Designing incentive systems is a challenge, but the dangers of incentive misalignment are great. You need your direct reports to act as agents for you, whether they're undertaking individual responsibilities or collective ones. You don't want to give them incentives to pursue individual goals when true teamwork is necessary, or vice versa.

Articulate Your Vision

When you're aligning your team, don't forget about the organization's vision. After all, it's a key reason why you and your team come to work every day.

An inspiring vision has the following attributes:

- It taps into sources of inspiration. It is built on a foundation of intrinsic motivators, such as teamwork and contribution to society. One orthopedic medical device company, for example, had "Restoring the joy of motion" as its vision statement, accompanied by stories about injured athletes being able to compete again, and grandparents being able to hold their grandkids.

- It makes people part of "the story." The best statements of vision connect people to a larger narrative that provides meaning—for example, a quest to recapture the organization's past glories.

- It contains evocative language. The vision must describe in graphic terms what the organization will achieve and how people will feel to have achieved it. Launching twelve rockets in ten years is a goal; putting a man on the moon and returning him safely to Earth by the end of the decade, as President John F. Kennedy put it, is a vision.

Use the categories in table 7-2 to help craft your shared vision. Keep asking yourself, Why should people feel inspired to expend extra effort to achieve the goals we have defined for the organization?

TABLE 7-2

Inspirations for vision statements

Feeling committed?	**Achieving great results?**
• Commitment to an ideal • Sacrifice to realize the ideal	• Drive for excellence, quality, and continuous improvement • Provide challenging opportunities
Making a contribution?	**Being part of a team?**
• Service to customers and suppliers • Create a better society and a better world	• Teamwork and constant concern for the good of the team • A climate that emphasizes personally rewarding work in groups
Promoting individual growth?	**Having control of one's destiny?**
• Respect for the individual, expressed as elimination of exploitative or patronizing practices • Provide the means for people to reach their potential	• Quest to be dominant and in control • Rewards, recognition, and status—individually and for the organization
Embodying trust and integrity?	
• Ethical and honest behavior • Fairness	

As you work to create and communicate a shared vision, keep the following principles in mind:

- **Use consultation to gain commitment.** Be clear on which elements of your vision are nonnegotiable, but beyond these, be flexible enough to consider the ideas of others and allow them to have input and to influence the shared vision. In that way, they share ownership. Off-site meetings are often a powerful way to create and generate commitment to a shared vision, as long as you take care to ensure they are well designed. (See box, "Off-Site Planning Checklist.")

- **Develop stories and metaphors to communicate it.** Stories and metaphors are potent ways to communicate the essence of a vision. There is something surprisingly powerful in a parable. The best of these stories crystallize core lessons and provide models for the kind of behavior you want to encourage.

- **Reinforce it.** Research on persuasive communication heavily underlines the power of repetition. Your vision is more likely to take root in people's minds if it consists of a few core themes that are repeated until they sink in. Even when people have begun to understand the message, you should not stop. Strive constantly to deepen people's commitment to the vision.

- **Develop channels for communicating it.** You cannot hope to communicate your vision directly to each person in your organization. This means that in addition to working with small groups such as a top team, you must be effective in persuading from a distance. This means developing communication channels that you will use to spread your vision more broadly.

Finally, and above all, take care to live the vision you articulate. A vision that is undercut by inconsistent leadership behaviors—by you or members of your team—is worse than no vision at all. Be sure you are prepared to walk the talk.

Off-site Planning Checklist

Before you schedule an off-site meeting for your new team, you need to clarify the reasons for doing so. What are you trying to accomplish with this meeting? There are at least six important reasons for having off-site meetings:

- To gain a shared understanding of the business (diagnostic focus)
- To define the vision and create a strategy (strategy focus)
- To change the way the team works together (team-process focus)
- To build or alter relationships in the group (relationship focus)
- To develop a plan and commit to achieving it (planning focus)
- To address conflicts and negotiate agreements (conflict-resolution focus)

Getting Down to Details

If you decide that an off-site meeting would indeed be useful for the group, start to consider the logistics of the meeting based on your answers to the following questions:

- When and where should the meeting be held?
- Which issues will be dealt with, and in what order?
- Who should act as facilitator?

Don't neglect the facilitation question. If you are a skilled facilitator and if the team respects you—and is not enmeshed in a conflict—it may make sense for you to be both leader and facilitator. If not, you'd be well advised to bring in a skilled outsider—either an expert on the substance of the issues you're dealing with or a skilled orchestrator of team process.

Avoiding the Traps

Don't try to do too much in a single off-site meeting. You can't realistically accomplish more than two of the goals outlined earlier in a day or two. Target a few, and stay focused.

Don't put the cart before the horse. You can't try to define the vision and create a strategy without first establishing the right foundation: a shared understanding of the business environment (diagnostic focus) and workplace relationships (relationship focus).

Leading Your Team

As you make progress in assessing, evolving, and aligning the team, think, too, about how you want to work with the team on a day-to-day, week-to-week basis. What processes will you use to shape how the team gets its collective job done? Teams vary strikingly in how they handle meetings, make decisions, resolve conflicts, and divide responsibilities and tasks. You will probably want to introduce new ways of doing things, but take care not to plunge into this task precipitously. First, familiarize yourself thoroughly with how your team worked before your arrival and how effective its processes were. In that way, you can preserve what worked well and change what did not.

Assess Your Team's Existing Processes

How can you quickly get a handle on your team's existing processes? Talk to team members, peers, and your boss about how the team worked. Read meeting minutes and team reports. Probe for answers to the following questions:

- **Participants' roles.** Who exerted the most influence on key issues? Did anyone play devil's advocate? Was there an innovator? Someone who avoided uncertainty? To whom did everyone else listen most attentively? Who was the peacemaker? The rabble-rouser?

- **Team meetings.** How often did your team meet? Who participated? Who set the agendas for meetings?

- **Decision making.** Who made what kinds of decisions? Who was consulted on decisions? Who was told after decisions were made?

- **Leadership style.** What leadership style did your predecessor prefer? That is, how did he prefer to learn, communicate, motivate, and handle decisions? How does your predecessor's leadership style compare with yours? If your styles differ markedly, how will you address the likely impact of those differences on your team?

Target Team Processes for Change

Once you grasp how your team functioned in the past—and what did and did not work well—use what you learn to establish the new processes you judge necessary. Many leaders decide, for example, that their team's meeting and decision-making processes would benefit from revision. If this is true of you, begin spelling out in specific terms what changes you envision. How often will the team meet? Who will attend which meetings? How will agendas be established and circulated? Setting up clear and effective processes will help your team coalesce and secure some early wins as a group.

Alter the Participants

One common team dysfunction—and a great opportunity to send a message that change is coming—concerns who participates in core team meetings. In some organizations, key meetings are too inclusive, with too many people participating in discussions and decision making. If this is the case, then reduce the size of the core group and streamline the meetings, sending the message that you value efficiency and focus. In other organizations, key meetings are too exclusive, with people who have potentially important opinions and information being systematically excluded. If this is the case, then judiciously broaden participation, sending the message that you will not play favorites or listen to only a few points of view.

Lead Decision Making

Decision making is another fertile area for potential improvement. Few leaders do a great job of leading team decision making. In part, this is because different types of decisions call for different decision-making processes, but most team leaders stick with one approach. They do this because they have a style with which they are comfortable and because they believe they need to be consistent or risk confusing their direct reports.

Research suggests that this view is wrongheaded.[3] The key is to have a framework for understanding and communicating why different decisions will be approached in different ways.

Think of the different ways teams can make decisions. Possible approaches can be arrayed on a spectrum ranging from unilateral decision making at one end to unanimous consent at the other. In unilateral decision making, the leader simply makes the call, either without consultation or with limited consultation with personal advisers. The risks associated with this approach are obvious: you may miss critical information and insights and get only lukewarm support for implementation.

At the other extreme, processes that require unanimous consent from more than a few people tend to suffer from *decision diffusion*. They go on and on, never reaching closure. Or, if a decision does get made, it is often a lowest-common-denominator compromise. In either case, critical opportunities and threats are not addressed effectively.

Between these two extremes are the decision-making processes that most leaders use: *consult-and-decide* and *build consensus*. When a leader solicits information and advice from direct reports—individually, as a group, or both—but reserves the right to make the final call, she is using a consult-and-decide approach. In effect she separates the "information gathering and analysis" process from the "evaluating and reaching closure" process, harnessing the group for one but not the other.

In the build-consensus process, the leader both seeks information and analysis and seeks buy-in from the group for any decision. The goal is not full consensus but sufficient consensus. This means that a critical mass of the group believes the decision to be the right one and, critically, that the rest agree they can live with and support implementation of the decision.

When should you choose one process over the other? The answer is emphatically not "If I am under time pressure, I will use consult-and-decide." Why? Because even though you may reach a decision more quickly by the consult-and-decide route, you won't necessarily reach the desired outcome faster. In fact, you may end up consuming a lot of time trying to sell the decision after the fact, or finding out that people are not energetically implementing it and having to pressure them. Those who suffer from the action imperative are most at risk of this; they want to reach closure by making the call but may jeopardize their end goals in the process.

The following rules of thumb can help you figure out which decision-making process to use:

- If the decision is likely to be highly divisive—creating winners and losers—then you usually are better off using consult-and-decide and taking the heat. A build-consensus process will fail to reach a good outcome and will get everyone mad at one another in the process. Put another way, decisions about sharing losses or pain among a group of people are best made by the leader.

- If the decision requires energetic support for implementation from people whose performance you cannot adequately observe and control, then you usually are better off using a build-consensus process. You may get to a decision more quickly using consult-and-decide, but you may not get the desired outcome.

- If your team members are inexperienced, then you usually are better off relying more on consult-and-decide until you've taken the measure of the team and developed their capabilities. If you try to adopt a build-consensus approach with an inexperienced team, you risk getting frustrated and imposing a decision anyway, and that undercuts teamwork.

- If you're put in charge of a group with whom you
  need to establish your authority (such as supervis-
  ing former peers), then you're better off relying on
  consult-and-decide to make some key early decisions.
  You can relax and rely more on building consensus
  once people see that you have the steadiness and
  insight to make tough calls.

Your approach to decision making will also vary depending
on which of the STARS situations you're in. In start-ups and
turnarounds, consult-and-decide often works well. The problems
tend to be technical (markets, products, technologies) rather than
cultural and political. Also, people may be hungry for "strong"
leadership, which often is associated with a consult-and-decide
style. To be effective in realignment and sustaining-success situations, in contrast, leaders often need to deal with strong, intact
teams and confront cultural and political issues. These sorts of
issues are typically best addressed with the build-consensus
approach.

To alter your approach to decision making depending on the
nature of the decision to be made, you will sometimes have to
restrain your natural inclinations. You are likely to have a preference for either consult-and-decide or build-consensus decision
making. But preferences are not destiny. If you are a consult-and-
decide person, you should consider experimenting with building
(sufficient) consensus in suitable situations. If you are a build-
consensus person, you should feel free to adopt a consult-and-
decide approach when it is appropriate to do so.

To avoid confusion, consider explaining to your direct reports
what process you're using and why. More importantly, strive to
run a fair process.[4] Even if people do not agree with the final
decision, they often will support it if they feel (1) that their views

and interests have been heard and taken seriously and (2) that you have given them a plausible rationale for why you made the call you did. The corollary? Don't engage in a charade of consensus building—an effort to build support for a decision already made. This rarely fools anyone, and it creates cynicism and undercuts implementation. You are better off to simply use consult-and-decide.

Finally, you often can shift between build-consensus and consult-and-decide modes as you gain deeper insight into peoples' interests and positions. It may make sense, for example, to begin in a consensus-building mode but reserve the right to shift to consult-and-decide if the process is becoming too divisive. It also may make sense to begin with consult-and-decide and shift to build-consensus if it emerges that energetic implementation is critical and consensus is possible.

Adjust for Virtual Teams

Finally, how should you modify your approach to building your team if some or all of the members are working remotely? It's a big challenge to gain and sustain cohesion in virtual teams. It also makes it more difficult to evaluate team members, especially if the situation precludes early face-to-face meetings. Although most of the principles of effective teamwork apply to virtual teams, there are a few additional things to consider:

- **Bring the team together early if at all possible.** The technology to support virtual interactions is improving. However, if true teamwork is required, there still is no substitute for getting people together to establish a shared foundation of knowledge, relationships, alignment, and mutual commitment.

- **Establish clear norms about communication.** This includes which communication channels will be used and how they will be employed. It also means having explicit agreements concerning responsiveness—for example, that urgent messages will be responded to within a specified time. Often it's essential as well to have clear norms about how people will interact during virtual meetings—for example, interrupting less than usual when meeting face-to-face, but also being more efficient in putting points across.

- **Clearly define team support roles.** Virtual teams need to be more disciplined about capturing and sharing information as well as following up on commitments. It often helps to assign people specific team support roles (perhaps on a rotating basis), such as note-taker and agenda-creator.

- **Create a rhythm for team interaction.** Co-located teams naturally establish patterns and routines for interaction; these can be as simple as arriving at roughly the same time or talking over coffee. Virtual teams, especially those working in multiple time zones, lack natural opportunities to create these reassuring routines. Therefore, it's essential to provide a lot of structure for virtual team interaction—for example, setting meeting times and following specified agendas.

- **Don't forget to celebrate success.** It's easy for members of a virtual team to feel disconnected, especially if most of the team is co-located and only a few are working remotely. Although it's always important to pause occasionally to recognize and celebrate accomplishments, it's essential in virtual teams.

Jump-Starting the Team

Your decisions about the team you inherited probably will be the most important decisions you make. Done well, your effort to assess, evolve, align, and lead the team will pay dividends in the focus and energy people bring to achieving goals and securing early wins. You will know you've been successful in building your team when you reach the break-even point—when the energy the team creates is greater than the energy you need to put into it. It will take a while before that happens; you must charge the battery before you can start the engine.

BUILD YOUR TEAM—CHECKLIST

1. What are your criteria for assessing the performance of members of your team? How are relative weightings affected by functions, the extent of required teamwork, the STARS portfolio, and the criticality of the positions?

2. How will you go about assessing your team?

3. What personnel changes do you need to make? Which changes are urgent, and which can wait? How will you create backups and options?

4. How will you make high-priority changes? What can you do to preserve the dignity of the people affected? What help will you need with the team in the restructuring process, and where are you going to find it?

5. How will you align the team? What mix of push (goals, incentives) and pull (shared vision) will you use?

6. How do you want your new team to operate? What roles do you want people to play? Do you need to shrink the core team or expand it? How do you plan to manage decision making?

CHAPTER 8

Create Alliances

Four months into her new job at MedDev, Alexia Belenko already was deeply frustrated by the bureaucratic maneuvering going on at corporate headquarters. "Where's the support for needed change?" she wondered.

An accomplished sales and marketing professional, Alexia had risen through the country-management ranks of MedDev, a global medical devices company, to become the firm's managing director (also informally known as "country manager") in her native Russia.

Senior leaders recognized Alexia's potential and decided she needed broader regional experience. So they appointed her regional vice president of marketing for EMEA (Europe, the Middle East, and Africa). In this new role, Alexia was responsible for marketing strategy for MedDev's country operations in the region. Alexia reported directly to Marjorie Aaron, the senior vice president of corporate marketing, who was based at the company's U.S. headquarters, and Alexia had a dotted-line reporting relationship with her former boss, Harald Jaeger, the international vice president for EMEA operations, to whom all the managing directors in the region reported.

Alexia dove in with her usual enthusiasm. She conducted a thorough review of current affairs, including one-on-one conversations with managing directors across the EMEA region and with her former boss. She also traveled to the United States expressly to meet with Marjorie and a couple of Marjorie's direct reports.

Drawing on those discussions, as well as her own experiences in the field, Alexia concluded that the most pressing problems—and opportunities—lay in better managing the tension between centralizing and decentralizing marketing decisions for new-product launches. Alexia put together a business case, outlining her assessment and recommendations for increasing standardization in some areas (for example, decisions concerning overall brand identity and positioning) and giving the managing directors more flexibility in others (such as making important adjustments to advertising promotion plans).

Marjorie and Harald saw merits in Alexia's approach, but neither was prepared to commit. Both directed her to brief the key stakeholders: MedDev's corporate marketing executives in the United States, and the EMEA country managers.

Six weeks and many confounding meetings later, Alexia felt as if she was caught in quicksand. She had scheduled a meeting with important members of the corporate marketing team, including David Wallace, the executive reporting to Marjorie Aaron in charge of global branding. She then flew to the United States to present to a group of more than thirty people. Virtually every one of them had suggestions, all of which would result in more central control, not less.

She was surprised, too, when a conference call with the EMEA country managers—her old colleagues who reported to Harald Jaeger—didn't go much better. They were more than happy to accept any ideas Alexia had that would give them additional flexibility. But when there was any mention of more limits to their autonomy, members of the group rapidly closed ranks. One respected managing director, Rolf Eiklid, expressed concern that the flexibility they were being offered wouldn't be enough to compensate for what they would be giving up and that corporate wouldn't really honor agreements. "We've been promised more flexibility in the past, and it hasn't materialized," he said.

The usually sure-footed Alexia was thrown off her stride by this turn of events. She was left wondering whether she had the patience and finesse to navigate the politics of her new regional role.

To succeed in your new role, you will need the support of people over whom you have no direct authority. You may have little or no relationship capital at the outset, especially if you're onboarding into a new organization. So you will need to invest energy in building new networks. Start early. Discipline yourself to invest in building up "relationship bank accounts" with people you anticipate needing to work with later. Think hard about whether there are people you haven't met who are likely to be critical to your success.

Recognize, too, when a new role presents you with very different influence challenges from those you've experienced in the past. Alexia was used to operating with a lot of positional authority and a team that reported directly to her. She didn't recognize early enough that she needed to influence in very different ways—through persuasion and alliance building—than she had in the past.

Even if you have significant positional authority in your new role, however, you should focus on building support for your early-win objectives. This means figuring out whom you must influence, pinpointing who is likely to support (and who is likely to resist) your key initiatives, and persuading swing voters. Plans for doing this should be an integral part of your overall 90-day plan.

Defining Your Influence Objectives

The first step is to be clear about why you need the support of others. Start by thinking about the alliances you need to build in order to secure your early wins. For which of these wins will you need to gain the support of others over whom you have no (or insufficient) authority? Armed with a clear understanding of what you're trying to accomplish, you can drill down and figure out whose support is essential and how you will secure it. Consider creating an alliance-building plan of each of your early-win projects.

Alexia's main goal was to negotiate a new deal (a "grand bargain") between her new and old bosses and their respective organizations about the ways important marketing decisions would be made in EMEA. The status quo reflected a long-standing compromise between the two sides. It was an uneasy equilibrium, but more or less stable. And on the face of it, any changes were win-lose propositions. The corporate marketing organization naturally favored more centralization and standardization. The managing directors in the EMEA region wanted more local customization. The implication was that an agreement, if one could be found at all, would consist of a package of trades that both sides could support.

To secure such an agreement, Alexia needed to build supportive alliances within both sides. It was unlikely she'd be able to achieve complete unanimity, because some people would have too much invested in the status quo. So she should have focused instead on winning a critical mass of support for agreement in both the corporate and the regional organizations.

Had Alexia understood this from the start, she might have focused her initial efforts differently—not only on diagnosing problems and proposing rational solutions but also on understanding how her agenda fit into the broader political landscape on both sides of the Atlantic. She would not have assumed that the strength of her business case would carry the day, nor would she have felt compelled to win over every single stakeholder.

Instead, she should have identified the specific alliances she needed to build and then figured out how to exert the necessary influence in the organization. This process of mapping the influence landscape also might have helped her identify potential blockers: what or who might stand in the way of getting support for her direction? How could she get those in opposition to finally say yes?

Understanding the Influence Landscape

Armed with clarity on why you need to influence people, the next step is to identify who will be most important for your success. Who are the key decision makers? What do you need them to do, and when do you need them to do it? Table 8-1 provides a simple tool for capturing this information. Consider creating such a list for each early-win initiative you're pursuing.

TABLE 8-1

Identifying influential players

Start to map your influence landscape by identifying influential players, what you need them to do, and when you need them to do it.

Who	What	When

Win and Block Alliances

Next, for each of your early-win initiatives, ask yourself which decision makers are essential for things to move forward. Together, these people are your *winning alliances*—the set of people who collectively have the power to support your agenda.[1] Alexia, for instance, needed to secure approval for her proposals from Marjorie on the corporate side, and from Harald on the EMEA side. Together, they were the winning alliance Alexia needed to build.

It also pays to think hard about potential *blocking alliances*—those who collectively have the power to say no. Who might band together to try to block your agenda, and why? How might they seek to impede the process? If you have a good sense of where opposition might come from, you can work to neutralize it.

Map Influence Networks

Senior decision makers usually are influenced to a significant degree by the opinions of others on whom they rely for advice and counsel. So the next step is to map *influence networks*—who influences whom on the issues of concern to you. Influence networks can play a huge role in determining whether or not change ultimately happens. Formal authority is by no means the only source of power in organizations; people tend to defer to others' opinions when it comes to important issues and decisions. Marjorie, for example, may defer to David's assessment of the impact of increased local customization on brand identity. Likewise, Harald may defer to Rolf because he commands the respect of and represents his peers.

Influence networks are channels for communication and persuasion that operate in parallel with the formal structure—a sort of shadow organization.[2] Sometimes these informal channels support what the formal organization is trying to do; at other times, they act to subvert it. To achieve her objective, Alexia needed to map networks of influence within corporate marketing, as well as with her old colleagues in the EMEA regional organization.

How do you map influence networks? To a degree, they will become obvious as you get to know the organization—by, for example, working with your peers. But you can accelerate the process. One good way to start is by identifying the key points of contact between your organization and others. Customers and suppliers, within the business and outside, are natural focal points for alliance building.

Another strategy is to get your boss to connect you to key stakeholders. Request a list of the key people outside your group whom he thinks you should get to know. Then set up early meetings with them. (In the spirit of the golden rule of transitions, consider proactively doing the same thing when you have new direct reports coming on board: create priority relationship lists for them, and help them make contact.)

Take care, too, to observe carefully in meetings and other interactions to see who defers to whom on crucial issues. Notice whom people go to for advice and insight, and who shares what information and news. Who defers to whom when certain topics are being discussed? When an issue is raised, where do people's eyes track?

As you learn more, try to identify the sources of power that give particular people influence in the organization. Here are examples:

- Expertise

- Control of information

- Connections to others

- Access to resources, such as budgets and rewards

- Personal loyalty

Over time, the patterns of influence will become clearer, and you'll be able to identify those vital individuals—the opinion leaders—who exert disproportionate influence because of their informal authority, expertise, or sheer force of personality. If you convince them, broader acceptance of your ideas is likely to follow.

You will also begin to recognize the *power coalitions*: groups of people who explicitly or implicitly cooperate over the long term to pursue certain goals or protect certain privileges. Figuring out their agendas, and linking yours to them, can be a powerful way to build support, as long as you don't end up watering down what you're trying to do or get enmeshed in political machinations that could undercut you.

Draw Influence Diagrams

It can be instructive to summarize what you learn about patterns of influence by drawing an influence diagram like the one for Alexia's situation shown in figure 8-1.

At the center circle are the critical decision makers—Marjorie in corporate marketing and Harald in EMEA operations. Alexia needed both to agree with the proposed package of changes, so they jointly constituted a winning alliance. However, as the arrows in the diagram indicate, these two executives would be influenced by people within their own organizations. (Heavier arrows denote a greater degree of influence.) Marjorie would be strongly influenced by David, her vice

FIGURE 8-1

Alexia's influence diagram

This diagram illustrates the key influence relationships that will shape decision making on the issues Alexia Belenko is trying to address in her organization.

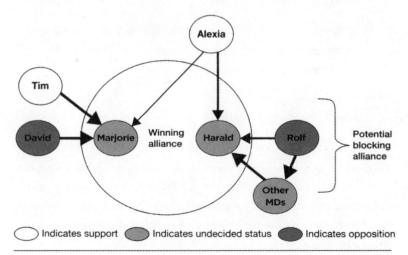

president of global branding, and Tim Marshall, vice president in the corporate strategy group. Harald would be influenced by the collective opinions of the country managers who report to him. But Rolf, the longtime managing director of the Nordic countries, would be highly influential both in shaping Harald's views and in influencing the other managing directors. The diagram also shows that Alexia herself had significant influence on Harald and some on Marjorie.

Identify Supporters, Opponents, and Persuadables

The work you've done to map influence networks in your organization can also help you pinpoint potential supporters, opponents, and persuadables. To identify your potential supporters, look for the following:

- People who share your vision for the future. If you see a need for change, look for others who have pushed for similar changes in the past.

- People who have been quietly working for change on a small scale, such as a plant engineer who has found an innovative way to significantly reduce waste.

- People new to the company who have not yet become acculturated to its mode of operation.

Whatever supporters' reasons for backing you, do not take their support for granted. It's never enough merely to identify support; you must solidify and nurture it. So don't forget to preach to the converted. Be sure, too, to ask supporters to be force multipliers by helping you influence others and by providing them with the most persuasive arguments for doing so.

As you look for support, be sure to identify people with whom you could build *alliances of convenience*. There will be individuals with whom you disagree in many areas, but with whom you align on the specific issue of concern. If this is the case, think hard about how to educate and enlist them.

Then there is the opposition. True adversaries will oppose you no matter what you do. They may believe you're wrong in your assessments of the situation. Or they may have other reasons for resistance to your agenda:

- **Comfort with the status quo.** They resist changes that might undermine their positions or alter established relationships.

- **Fear of looking incompetent.** They fear seeming or feeling incompetent if they have trouble adapting to the changes you're proposing and perform inadequately afterward.

- **Threats to core values.** They believe you're promoting a culture that spurns traditional definitions of value or rewards inappropriate behavior.

- **Threats to their power.** They fear that the change you're proposing (such as giving more decision rights to front-line managers) would deprive them of power.

- **Negative consequences for their allies.** They fear that your agenda will have negative consequences for others they care about or feel responsible for.

But be careful not to assume that people are adversaries. When you meet resistance, probe for the reasons behind it before labeling people as implacably opposed. Understanding resisters' motives many equip you to counter their arguments. For example, you may be able to address their fears of appearing incompetent in the new environment by helping them develop new skills.

Keep in mind, too, that success in winning over adversaries can have a powerful, symbolic impact. "The enemy who is converted to the ally" is a powerful story that will resonate with others in the organization. (Another example is the story of redemption—for example, helping a person who has been marginalized or labeled as ineffective prove himself.)

There also will be people with whom you have good relationships and agree on many issues but who are not aligned with your specific agenda. These are a special class of opposition, and the key here is to find ways to preserve these relationships while still moving things in needed directions. See if you can do this by explaining what you need to do and why, by engaging in constructive problem-solving, and perhaps by finding ways to make up for their losses by helping them with other issues or returning the favor later.

Finally, don't forget about the *persuadables*—those people in the organization who are indifferent or undecided or uncommitted about your plans but who might be persuaded to throw their support your way if you can figure out how to influence them. Once you have identified them, figure out why they're uncommitted. They may be:

- **Indifferent.** There may be many ways to get them to support your agenda in return for your support of theirs.

- **Undecided.** Find out why, and work to educate and persuade them.

- **Political operators waiting to see which way the wind will blow.** You need to convince them that things are going your way so that they climb on the bandwagon.

Your assessment of support and opposition can be summarized in your influence map, as illustrated earlier in figure 8-1. The darker circles indicate people who are opposed, light gray means they are supportive, and medium gray designates the undecided. (You also can use green-yellow-red color coding). On the corporate side in Alexia's situation, Tim was supportive, whereas David was undecided. On the EMEA side, Rolf was somewhat opposed to Alexia's proposed changes. Note that, once again, she had to win a critical mass of support on both sides for a deal to be struck.

Understanding Pivotal People

Now that you've analyzed the influence networks in your organization, identified the players and alliances, and mapped out support and opposition, the next step is to focus on the pivotal people you need to influence. In Alexia's case, these were David and Rolf.

Start by assessing their intrinsic motivators. People are motivated by various things, such as a need for recognition, for control, for power, for affiliation through relationships with colleagues, and for personal growth.[3] The relative weightings of these motivators can vary greatly. So take the time to figure out what makes the pivotal people tick. If it is possible to engage them directly in dialogue, ask questions and engage in active listening. Seek especially to understand what potential opponents like Rolf are opposed to, and why. Given what motivates them, are there specific losses they're trying to avoid? Is there something you can give them—a valuable trade—that might help compensate?

Understanding people's motivations is only part of the story. You also need to assess *situational pressures*: the driving and restraining forces acting on them because of the situation they're in. Driving forces push people in the direction you want them to go, and restraining forces are situational reasons they would say no. There is a lot of good social psychology research showing that we overestimate the impact of personality and underestimate the impact of situational pressures in reaching conclusions about the reasons people act the way they do.[4] Rolf's opposition could be rooted in intrinsic inflexibility and a need to preserve his power and status, or he could be responding to situational pressures such as his business goals and incentives or the opinions of his peers (or a combination). So take the time to think about the forces acting on the people you want to influence. Then find ways to increase the drive and remove some restraints.

Finally, think about how key people perceive their alternatives or choices. What are the options from which they believe they can choose? Critical here is to assess whether opponents like Rolf believe that resistance—overt or covert—can succeed in preserving the status quo. If so, then it could be important to convince them that the status quo is no longer a viable option. Once people perceive that change is going to happen, the game often shifts from outright opposition to a competition to influence what sort of change will occur. Could Alexia have convinced the key decision makers that the current situation was not acceptable, that change needed to take place?

Concerns about the implementation of agreements also fall into this category. People may believe that concessions offered by others will not really materialize and that they are better off fighting for the status quo than taking a chance. This seems to be one concern that Rolf was voicing when he expressed worries about whether corporate would honor agreements to give the managing directors more flexibility. If worries about insecure agreements turn out to be blocking progress, see whether there are ways you can increase the confidence level. For example, you might propose phasing in the changes, with each step linked to success in implementing the previous ones.

TABLE 8-2

Analyzing motivations, driving and restraining forces, and alternatives

Use this table to assess what motivates pivotal players, as well as the driving and restraining forces acting on them, and their perceptions of their alternatives (what choices they believe they have).

Pivot players	Motivations	Driving and restraining forces	Alternatives

Table 8-2 provides a simple tool for capturing information about motivations, driving and restraining forces, and perceptions of alternatives for pivotal people.

Crafting Influence Strategies

Armed with deeper insight into the people you need to influence, you can think about how to apply classic influence techniques such as consultation, framing, choice-shaping, social influence, incrementalism, sequencing, and action-forcing events.

Consultation promotes buy-in, and good consultation means engaging in active listening. You pose questions and encourage people to voice their real concerns, and then you summarize and feed back what you've heard. This approach signals that you're paying attention and taking the conversation seriously. The power of active listening as a persuasive technique is vastly underrated. It can not only promote acceptance of difficult decisions but also channel people's thinking and frame choices. Because the questions leaders ask and the ways they summarize responses have a powerful effect on people's perceptions, active listening and framing are a potent persuasive technique.

Framing means carefully crafting your persuasive arguments on a person-by-person basis. It's well worth the time to get your framing right. Indeed, if Alexia can't develop and communicate a compelling case in support of her proposed changes, nothing else she does will have much impact. Your messages should take an appropriate tone, resonate with the motivations of influential players and the forces acting on them, and, critically, shape how the key players perceive their alternatives.

Alexia, for example, should have explored what it would take to move Rolf from being opposed to at least being neutral and, ideally, supportive. Did he have specific concerns that she could have addressed? Was there a set of trades that he would have found attractive if implementation could have been guaranteed? Were there ways of helping him advance other agendas he cared about in exchange for his support of Alexia's approach?

As you frame your arguments, keep in mind Aristotle's rhetorical categories of *logos*, *ethos*, and *pathos*.[5] Logos is about making logical arguments—using data, facts, and reasoned rationales to build your case for change. Ethos is about elevating the principles that should be applied (such as fairness) and the values that must be upheld (such as a culture of teamwork) in making decisions. Pathos is about making powerful emotional connections with your audience—for example, putting forth an inspiring vision of what cooperation could accomplish.

Effective framing focuses on a few core themes, which are repeated until they sink in. It is a sure sign of success when people begin to echo your themes without knowing they're doing so.

Focus and repetition are effective because we learn through repetition. By the third or fourth time we hear a song, we can't get it out of our minds. It is possible, though, to hear a song so much that we get sick of it. Similarly, using precisely the same words over and over makes it apparent that you're trying to persuade, and that can provoke a backlash. The art of effective communication is to repeat and elaborate core themes without sounding like a parrot.

As you frame your arguments, think about how you can inoculate people against counterarguments you expect opponents to make. Presenting and decisively refuting weak forms of expected counterarguments immunizes audiences against the same arguments when they're advanced in more potent forms.

Table 8-3 provides a simple checklist for framing the types of arguments you need to make.

TABLE 8-3

Framing arguments

Use the following categories and questions to identify the types of arguments you need to make to convince people.

Logos—data and reasoned arguments	• What data or analysis might they find persuasive? • What logic(s) might appeal to them? • Are there biases to which they are falling prey and, if so, how might you demonstrate this?
Ethos—principles, policies, and other "rules"	• Are there principles or policies that they could be convinced should operate here? • If you are asking them to act counter to a principle or policy, can you help them justify making an exception?
Pathos—emotions and meaning	• Are there emotional "triggers," for example loyalty or contribution to the common good, to which you could appeal? • Can you help them create a sense of meaning by supporting or opposing a cause? • If they are reacting too emotionally, can you help them step back and get perspective?

Choice-shaping is about influencing how people perceive their alternatives. Think hard about how to make it hard to say no. Sometimes choices are best posed broadly, at other times more narrowly. If you're asking someone to support something that could be seen as setting an undesirable precedent, it might best be framed as a highly circumscribed, isolated situation independent of other decisions. Other choices might be better situated within the context of a higher-level set of issues.

Selling choices perceived as win-lose propositions is particularly difficult. Broadening the range of issues or options under consideration can facilitate mutually beneficial trades that enlarge the pie. Progress likewise can be stalled by the presence of toxic issues. These sometimes can be neutralized by explicitly setting them aside for future consideration or by making up-front commitments that allay anxieties.

Social influence is the impact of the opinions of others and the rules of the societies in which they live. The knowledge that a highly respected person already supports an initiative alters others' assessments of its attractiveness. So convincing opinion leaders to make commitments of support and to mobilize their own networks can have a powerful leveraging effect. Likewise, research suggests that people prefer to operate in these ways:

- **Remain consistent with strongly held values and beliefs.** These values tend to be shared with important reference groups. People asked to engage in behavior inconsistent with their values or beliefs experience internal psychological dissonance.

- **Remain consistent with their prior commitments and decisions.** Failure to honor commitments tends to incur social sanctions, and inconsistency is a signal of unreliability. People prefer not to make choices that require them to reverse themselves or that overtly constrain their future choices by setting undesirable precedents.

- **Repay obligations.** Reciprocity is a strong social norm, and people are vulnerable to appeals for support that invoke past favors they've received.

- **Preserve their reputations.** Choices that preserve or enhance one's reputation are viewed favorably, whereas those that could jeopardize one's reputation are viewed negatively.

The implication is that you need to avoid, to the extent possible, asking others to make choices that are inconsistent with their values and prior commitments, decrease their status, threaten their reputations, or risk evoking the disapproval of respected others. If someone you need to influence has a competing prior commitment, you should look for ways to help them gracefully escape from it.

Incrementalism refers to the notion that people can move in desired directions step-by-step when they wouldn't go in a single leap. Mapping out a pathway from A to B is highly effective, because each small step taken creates a new psychological reference point for people in deciding whether to take the next one. For instance, Alexia could have started by meeting with people just to explore the centralization-versus-flexibility problem. Over time, however, the group could have analyzed each of the issues involved. And finally, after they had deliberately walked through all major concerns, the participants could have discussed basic principles for what a good solution might look like.

Getting people involved in shared diagnosis of organizational problems is a form of incrementalism: involvement in the diagnosis makes it difficult for people to deny the need for tough decisions. Once there is agreement on the problem, you can shift to defining the options and then the criteria that will be used to evaluate them.

By the end of such a process, people are often willing to accept outcomes they would never have accepted at the outset.

Because incrementalism can have a powerful impact, it's essential to influence decision making before momentum builds in the wrong direction. Decision-making processes are like rivers: big decisions draw on preliminary tributary processes that define the problem, identify alternatives, and establish criteria for evaluating costs and benefits. By the time the problem and the options have been defined, the actual choice may be a foregone conclusion. So remember that early success in shaping the process can have a big impact on the eventual outcome.

Sequencing means being strategic about the order in which you seek to influence people to build momentum in desired directions.[6] If you approach the right people first, you can set in motion a virtuous cycle of alliance building. Success in gaining one respected ally makes it easier to recruit others—and your resource base increases. With broader support, the likelihood increases that your agenda will succeed, making it easier still to recruit more supporters. Based on her assessment of patterns of influence at MedDev, for example, Alexia definitely should have met first with corporate strategy VP Tim Marshall to solidify his support and arm him with additional information for persuading Marjorie.

More generally, Alexia's sequencing plan would consist of a well-thought-through series of one-on-one and group meetings to create the momentum for change. The critical point here is getting the mix right. One-on-one meetings are effective for getting the lay of the land—for instance, hearing people's positions, shaping their views by providing new or extra information, or potentially negotiating side deals. But the participants in a serious negotiation often aren't willing to make their final concessions and commitments unless they're sitting face-to-face with others, and that is when group meetings are particularly effective.

Action-forcing events get people to stop deferring decisions, delaying, and avoiding commitment of scarce resources. When your success requires the coordinated action of many people, delay by a single individual can have a cascade effect, giving others an excuse not to proceed. You must therefore eliminate inaction as an option.

You do this by setting up action-forcing events—events that induce people to make commitments or take actions. Meetings, review sessions, teleconferences, and deadlines can all help create and sustain momentum: regular meetings to review progress, and tough questioning of those who fail to reach agreed-to goals, increase the psychological pressure to follow through.

Putting It All Together

Alliance building entails figuring out whose support you need, mapping the patterns of influence, and identifying potential support and opposition. Success in these actions helps you identify pivotal people, understand their motivations, situational pressures, and perceptions of the alternatives, and craft the right strategies to build your winning alliances.

CREATE ALLIANCES—CHECKLIST

1. What are the critical alliances you need to build—both within your organization and externally—to advance your agenda?

2. What agendas are other key players pursuing? Where might they align with yours, and where might they come into conflict?

3. Are there opportunities to build long-term, broad-based alliances with others? Where might you be able to leverage shorter-term agreements to pursue specific objectives?

4. How does influence work in the organization? Who defers to whom on key issues of concern?

5. Who is likely to support your agenda? Who is likely to oppose you? Who is persuadable?

6. What are the motivations of pivotal people, the situational pressures acting on them, and their perceptions of their choices?

7. What are the elements of an effective influence strategy? How should you frame your arguments? Might influence tools such as incrementalism, sequencing, and action-forcing events help?

CHAPTER 9

Manage Yourself

After six great years in the New York office of a large media company, Stephen Erikson was promoted to a senior position at the firm's Canadian unit. He expected the move from New York to Toronto to be a breeze. After all, Canadians and Americans are pretty much alike. And the city was safe and reputed to have good restaurants and cultural events.

Stephen moved right away, rented a short-term apartment in downtown Toronto, and dove into the new job with his usual energy. His wife, Irene, an accomplished freelance interior designer, put up their co-op apartment for sale and started preparing their two children—Katherine, twelve, and Elizabeth, nine—for a move in the middle of the school year. Stephen and Irene had talked about postponing moving the children until the end of the school year, four months away, but decided it was too long to have the family separated.

The first hints of trouble in the new job were subtle. Every time he tried to get something done, Stephen felt as if he was wading through molasses. As a lifelong New Yorker accustomed to bluntness in talking about business, he found his new colleagues irritatingly polite and "nice." Stephen complained to Irene that his colleagues refused to engage in hardheaded discussions about the tough issues. And he couldn't find the kind of go-to people he had relied on to get things done in New York.

Four weeks after Stephen started the job, Irene joined him in Toronto to look for a new house and school and to scope out prospects for continuing her freelance design work. Stephen was frustrated with the job and irritable. Irene's unhappiness quickly mounted when she couldn't find schools to her liking. The children had been happily enrolled in a top-tier private school in New York. They were displeased about moving and had been making Irene's life miserable. She had calmed them with stories about the adventure of moving to a new country and promises to find them a great new school. Dispirited, she told Stephen she thought they should leave the kids where they were until the end of the year; he agreed.

With Stephen commuting between Toronto and New York, and Irene under pressure as a working single parent, events quickly took their toll. Although Irene visited Toronto for a couple of weekends and continued looking into schools, it became clear that her heart was not in the move. Weekends often were stressful, with the children happy to see Stephen but unhappy about the move. Stephen often arrived back in the office on Mondays tired and found it hard to concentrate, aggravating his difficulties in getting traction and connecting with his colleagues and team. He knew his work performance was suffering, and that further increased his stress.

Eventually he decided to force the issue. Through connections at the company, he found a good school and identified some promising housing prospects. But when he pressed Irene to get going on selling their apartment, the result was the worst fight of their marriage. When it became clear their relationship was being jeopardized, Stephen told the firm he needed either to return to New York or quit.

The life of a leader is always a balancing act, but never more so than during a transition. The uncertainty and ambiguity can be crippling. You don't know what you don't know. You haven't had a chance to build a support network. If you've moved, as Stephen did, you're also in transition personally. If you have a family, they, too, are in transition. Amid all this turmoil, you're expected to get acclimated quickly and begin to effect positive change in your new organization. For all these reasons, managing yourself is a key transition challenge.

Are you focusing on the right things in the right way? Are you maintaining your energy and keeping your perspective? Are you and your family getting the support you need? Don't try to go it alone.

Taking Stock

A good place to start is to take stock of how you're feeling about how things are going in your transition right now. So take a few minutes to look at the "Guidelines for Structured Reflection" (see box) to assess how you're doing.

Guidelines for Structured Reflection

How Do You Feel So Far?

On a scale of high to low, do you feel:

- Excited? If not, why not? What can you do about it?
- Confident? If not, why not? What can you do about it?
- In control of your success? If not, why not? What can you do about it?

What Has Bothered You So Far?

- With whom have you failed to connect? Why?
- Of the meetings you've attended, which has been the most troubling? Why?
- Of all that you've seen or heard, what has disturbed you most? Why?

What Has Gone Well or Poorly?

- Which interactions would you handle differently if you could? Which exceeded your expectations? Why?
- Which of your decisions have turned out particularly well? Not so well? Why?
- What missed opportunities do you regret most? Was a better result blocked primarily by you, or by something beyond your control?

Now focus on the biggest challenges or difficulties you face. Be honest with yourself. Are your difficulties situational, or do their sources lie within you? Even experienced and skilled people may blame problems on the situation rather than on their own actions. The net effect is that they are less proactive than they could be.

Now take a step back. If things are not going completely the way you want, why is that? Is it only the inevitable emotional roller coaster you will experience when taking a new role? It's inevitable that your initial enthusiasm will wane as the excitement of taking on a new challenge wears off and the reality sets in of the challenges you face. It's common for leaders to go into a valley three to six months after taking a new role. The good news is that you're virtually certain to come out the other side—as long as you're applying your 90-day plan, of course.

It's also possible, however, that the difficulties you face are the result of deeper personal vulnerabilities that could take you off-track. That's because transitions tend to amplify your weaknesses. So look at the following list of potentially dysfunctional behaviors, and ask yourself (and, if it's safe to do so, others who know you well and will give you honest feedback) whether you potentially are suffering from any of these syndromes.

- **Undefended boundaries.** If you fail to establish solid boundaries defining what you are willing and not willing to do, the people around you—bosses, peers, and direct reports—will take whatever you have to give. The more you give, the less they will respect you and the more they will ask of you—another vicious cycle. Eventually you will feel angry and resentful that you're being nibbled to death, but you will have no one to blame but yourself. If you cannot establish boundaries for yourself, you cannot expect others to do it for you.

- **Brittleness.** The uncertainty inherent in transitions can exacerbate rigidity and defensiveness, especially in new leaders with a high need for control. Often the result is overcommitment to failing courses of action. You make a call prematurely and then feel unable to back away from it without losing credibility. The longer you wait, the harder it is to admit you were wrong, and the more calamitous the consequences. Or perhaps you decide that your way of accomplishing a particular goal is the only way. As a result, your rigidity disempowers people who have equally valid ideas about how to achieve the same goal.

- **Isolation.** To be effective, you must be connected to the people who make action happen and to the subterranean flow of information. It's surprisingly easy for new leaders to end up isolated, and isolation can creep up on you. It happens because you don't take the time to make the right connections, perhaps by relying overmuch on a few people or on official information. It also happens if you unintentionally discourage people from sharing critical information with you. Perhaps they fear your reaction to bad news, or they see you as having been captured by competing interests. Whatever the reason, isolation breeds uninformed decision making, which damages your credibility and further reinforces your isolation.

- **Work avoidance.** You will have to make tough calls early in your new job. Perhaps you must make major decisions about the direction of the business based on incomplete information. Or perhaps your personnel decisions will have a profound impact on people's lives. Consciously or unconsciously, you may choose to delay by burying yourself in other work or fool yourself into believing that the time isn't ripe to make the call. The result is what leadership thinkers have termed *work avoidance*: the tendency to avoid taking the bull by the horns, which results in tough problems becoming even tougher.[1]

All these syndromes can contribute to dangerous levels of stress. Not all stress is bad. In fact, there is a well-documented relationship between stress and performance known as the Yerkes-Dodson curve, illustrated in figure 9-1.[2] Whether stress is self-generated or externally imposed, you need some stress (often in the form of positive incentives or consequences from inaction) to be productive. Without it, not much happens—you stay in bed munching chocolates.

FIGURE 9-1

Yerkes-Dodson human performance curve

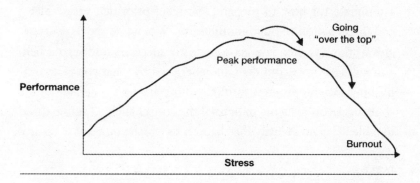

As you begin to experience pressure, your performance improves, at least at first. Eventually you reach a point (which varies from person to person) at which further demands, in the form of too many balls to juggle or too heavy an emotional load, start to undermine your performance. This dynamic creates more stress, further reducing your performance and creating a vicious cycle as you go over the top of your stress curve. Rarely, exhaustion sets in and you burn out. Much more common is chronic underperformance: you work harder and achieve less. This is what happened to Stephen.

Understanding the Three Pillars of Self-Management

If you have these sorts of weaknesses, what can you do about it? You must vigorously engage in self-management, a personal practice that is built on a foundation with three pillars. The first pillar is adoption of the success strategies presented in the previous eight chapters. The second pillar is creation and enforcement of some personal disciplines. The third pillar is formation of support systems, at work and at home, that help you maintain your balance.

Pillar 1: Adopt 90-Day Strategies

The strategies spelled out in the previous eight chapters represent a template for how to prepare, learn, set priorities, create plans, and direct action to build momentum. When you see these strategies work and when you get some early successes under your belt, you will feel more confident and energized by what you're accomplishing. As you progress through your transition, think about the challenges you're facing in light of the core challenges summarized in table 9-1, and identify the chapters to which you want to return.

TABLE 9-1

Assessment of core challenges

Core challenge	Diagnostic questions
Prepare yourself.	Are you adopting the right mind-set for your new job and letting go of the past?
Accelerate your learning.	Are you figuring out what you need to learn, whom to learn it from, and how to speed up the learning process?
Match your strategy to the situation.	Are you diagnosing the type of transition you face and the implications for what to do and what not to do?
Negotiate success.	Are you building your relationship with your new boss, managing expectations, and marshaling the resources you need?
Secure early wins.	Are you focusing on the vital priorities that will advance your long-term goals and build your short-term momentum?
Achieve alignment.	Are you identifying and fixing frustrating misalignments of strategy, structure, systems, and skills?
Build your team.	Are you assessing, restructuring, and aligning your team to leverage what you're trying to accomplish?
Create alliances.	Are you building a base of internal and external support for your initiatives so that you're not pushing rocks uphill?

Pillar 2: Develop Personal Disciplines

Knowing what you should be doing is not the same thing as doing it. Ultimately, success or failure emerges from the accumulation of daily choices that propel you in productive directions or push you off a cliff. This is the territory of the second pillar of personal efficacy: personal disciplines.

Personal disciplines are the regular routines you enforce on yourself ruthlessly. What specific disciplines are the highest priorities for you? It depends on what your strengths and weaknesses are. You may have a great deal of insight into yourself, but you should also consult others who know you well and whom you trust. (Some 360-degree feedback can be useful here.) What do they see as your strengths and, crucially, your potential weak spots?

Use the following list of personal disciplines to stimulate your thinking about routines you need to develop.

Plan to Plan. Do you devote time daily and weekly to a plan-work-evaluate cycle? If not, or if you do so irregularly, you need to be more disciplined about planning. At the end of each day, spend ten minutes evaluating how well you met your goals and then planning for the next day. Do the same thing at the end of each week. Get into the habit of doing this. Even if you fall behind, you will be more in control.

Focus on the Important. Do you devote time each day to the most important work that needs to be done? It's easy for the urgent to crowd out the important. You get caught up in the flow of transactions—phone calls, meetings, e-mail—and never find time to focus on the medium term, let alone the long term. If you're having trouble getting the real work done, discipline yourself to set aside a particular time each day, even as little as half an hour, when you will close the door, turn off your phone, ignore e-mail, and focus, focus, focus.

Judiciously Defer Commitment. Do you make commitments on the spur of the moment and later regret them? Do you blithely agree to do things in the seemingly remote future, only to kick yourself when the day arrives and your schedule is full? If you do, you must learn to defer commitment. Whenever anybody asks you to do something, say, "Sounds interesting. Let me think about it and get back to you." Never say yes on the spot. If you're being pressed (perhaps by someone who knows your vulnerability to such pressure), say, "Well, if you need an answer now, I'll have to say no. But if you can wait, I will give it more thought." Begin with no; it's easy to say yes later. It's difficult (and damaging to your reputation) to say yes and then change your mind. Keep in mind that people will ask you to make commitments far in advance, knowing that your schedule will look deceptively open.

Go to the Balcony. Do you find yourself getting too caught up in emotional escalation in difficult situations? If you do, discipline yourself to stand back, take stock from fifty thousand feet, and then make productive interventions. Leading authorities in the fields of leadership and negotiation have long praised the value of "going to the balcony" in this way.[3] It can be tough to do this, especially when the stakes are high and you're emotionally involved. But with discipline and practice, it is a skill that can be cultivated.

Check In with Yourself. Are you as aware as you need to be of your reactions to events during your transition? If not, discipline yourself to engage in structured reflection about your situation. For some new leaders, structured self-assessment means jotting down a few thoughts, impressions, and questions at the end of each day. For others, it means setting aside time each week to assess how things are going. Find an approach that suits your style, and discipline yourself to use it regularly. Work to translate the resulting insights into action.

Recognize When to Quit. To adapt an old saw, transitions are marathons and not sprints. If you find yourself going over the top of your stress curve more than occasionally, you must discipline yourself to know when to quit. This is easy to say and hard to do, of course, especially when you're up against a deadline and think one more hour might make all the difference. It may, in the short term, but the long-term cost could be steep. Work hard at recognizing when you're at the point of diminishing returns, and take a break of whatever sort refreshes you.

Pillar 3: Build Your Support Systems

The third pillar of self-management is solidifying your personal support systems. This means asserting control in your local environment, stabilizing the home front, and building a solid advice-and-counsel network.

Assert Control Locally. It's hard to focus on work if the basic infrastructure that supports you is not in place. Even if you have more pressing worries, move quickly to get your new office set up, develop routines, clarify expectations with your assistant, and so on. If necessary, assemble a set of temporary resources to tide you over until the permanent systems are operational.

Stabilize the Home Front. It's a fundamental rule of warfare to avoid fighting on too many fronts. For new leaders, this means stabilizing the home front so that you can devote the necessary attention to work. You cannot hope to create value at work if you're destroying value at home. This is the fundamental mistake that Stephen made.

If your new position involves relocation, your family is also in transition. Like Irene, your spouse may be making a job transition, too, and your children may have to leave their friends and change schools. In other words, the fabric of your family's life may be disrupted just when you most need support and stability. The stresses of your professional transition can amplify the strain of your family's transition. Also, family members' difficulties can add to your already heavy emotional load, undermining your ability to create value and lengthening the time it takes for you to reach the break-even point.

So focus on accelerating the family transition, too. The starting point is to acknowledge that your family may be unhappy, even resentful, about the transition. There is no avoiding disruption, but it can be helpful to talk about it and work through the sense of loss together.

Beyond that, here are some guidelines that can help smooth your family's transition:

- **Analyze your family's existing support system.** Moving severs your ties with the people who provide essential services for your family: doctors, lawyers, dentists, babysitters, tutors, coaches, and more. Do a support-system inventory, identify priorities, and invest in finding replacements quickly.

- **Get your spouse back on track.** Your spouse may quit his old job with the intention of finding a new one after relocating. Unhappiness can fester if the search is slow.

To accelerate it, negotiate up front with your company for job-search support, or find such support shortly after moving. Above all, don't let your spouse defer getting going.

- **Time the family move carefully.** For children, it is substantially more difficult to move in the middle of a school year. Consider waiting until the end of the school year to move your family. The price, of course, is separation from your loved ones and the wear and tear of commuting. If you do this, however, be sure that your spouse has extra support to help ease the burden. Being a single parent is hard work.

- **Preserve the familiar.** Reestablish familiar family rituals as quickly as possible, and maintain them throughout the transition. Help from favorite relatives, such as grandparents, also makes a difference.

- **Invest in cultural familiarization.** If you move internationally, get professional advice about the cross-cultural transition. Isolation is a far greater risk for your family if there are language and cultural barriers.

- **Tap into your company's relocation service, if it has one, as soon as possible.** Corporate relocation services are typically limited to helping you find a new home, move belongings, and locate schools, but such help can make a big difference.

There is no avoiding pain if you decide to move your family. But there is much you can do to minimize it and to accelerate everyone's transitions.

Build Your Advice-and-Counsel Network. No leader, no matter how capable and energetic, can do it all. You need a network of trusted advisers within and outside the organization with whom to talk through what you're experiencing. Your network is an indispensable resource that can help you avoid becoming isolated and losing perspective. As a starting point, you need to cultivate three types of advisers: technical advisers, cultural interpreters, and political counselors (see table 9-2).

You also need to think hard about the mix of internal and external advisers you want to cultivate. Insiders know the

TABLE 9-2

Types of advisers

Type	Role	How they help you
Technical advisers	Provide expert analysis of technologies, markets, and strategy	They suggest applications for new technologies. They interpret technical data and provide analysis. They provide timely and accurate information.
Cultural interpreters	Help you understand the new culture and (if that is your objective) adapt to it	They provide you with insight into cultural norms, mental models, and guiding assumptions. They help you learn to speak the language of the new organization.
Political counselors	Help you deal with political relationships within your new organization	They help you implement the advice of your technical advisers. They serve as a sounding board as you think through options for implementing your agenda. They challenge you with what-if questions.

organization, its culture and politics. Seek out people who are well connected and whom you can trust to help you grasp what is really going on. They are a priceless resource.

At the same time, insiders cannot be expected to give you dispassionate or disinterested views of events. Thus, you should augment your internal network with outside advisers and counselors who will help you work through the issues and decisions you face. They should be skilled at listening and asking questions, have good insight into the way organizations work, and have your best interests at heart.

Use table 9-3 to assess your advice-and-counsel network. Analyze each person in terms of the domains in which she assists you—technical adviser, cultural interpreter, political counselor—as well as whether each is an insider or an outsider.

Now take a step back. Will your existing network provide the support you need in your new role? Don't assume that people who have been helpful in the past will continue to be helpful in your new situation. You will encounter different problems, and former advisers may not be able to help you in your new role. As you attain higher levels of responsibility, for example, the need for good political counsel typically increases dramatically.

TABLE 9-3

Assessment of your advice-and-counsel network

	Technical advisers	Cultural interpreters	Political counselors
Internal advisers and counselors (inside your new organization)			
External advisers and counselors (outside your new organization)			

You should also be thinking ahead. Because it takes time to develop an effective network, it's not too early to focus on what sort of network you will need in your *next* job. How will your needs for advice change?

To develop an effective support network, you need to make sure you have the right help and your support network is there when you need it. Does your support network have the following qualities?

- The right mix of technical advisers, cultural interpreters, and political counselors.

- The right mix of internal and external advisers. You want honest feedback from insiders *and* the dispassionate perspective of outside observers.

- External supporters who are loyal to you as an individual, not to your new organization or unit. Typically, these are long-standing colleagues and friends.

- Internal advisers who are trustworthy, whose personal agendas don't conflict with yours, and who offer straight and accurate advice.

- Representatives of key constituencies who can help you understand their perspectives. You do not want to restrict yourself to one or two points of view.

Staying on Track

You will have to fight to manage yourself every single day. Ultimately, your success or failure will flow from all the small choices you make along the way. These choices can create momentum—for the organization and for you—or they can result in vicious cycles that undermine your effectiveness. Your day-to-day actions during your transition establish the pattern for all that follows, not only for the organization but also for your personal efficacy and ultimately your well-being.

MANAGE YOURSELF—CHECKLIST

1. What are your greatest vulnerabilities in your new role? How do you plan to compensate for them?

2. What personal disciplines do you most need to develop or enhance? How will you do that? What will success look like?

3. What can you do to gain more control over your local environment?

4. What can you do to ease your family's transition? What support relationships will you have to build? Which are your highest priorities?

5. What are your priorities for strengthening your advice-and-counsel network? To what extent do you need to focus on your internal network? Your external network? In which domain do you most need additional support—technical, cultural, political, or personal?

CHAPTER 10

Accelerate Everyone

The First 90 Days was conceived as a book for individual leaders in transition. It was written to help them diagnose their situations, define the core challenges, and design plans to create momentum. Hundreds of thousands of leaders have benefited from the approach, which independent research has shown reduces time to break-even by as much as 40 percent.[1]

When a new leader fails to thrive, it's a severe, perhaps career-ending, blow to the individual. But what about the impact of transitions on companies? Every failed transition—whether outright derailment or less dramatic underperformance—exacts costs from the organization as well. The magnitude of these costs is such that a state-of-the-art transition acceleration system (hereafter "acceleration system") can reduce enterprise risk, create competitive advantage, and speed up change implementation.

Think first about the risks posed by senior executive transitions, both onboarding of new hires and internal promotions. A single failure at the senior executive level can cost hundreds of thousands of dollars in direct costs, never mind lost opportunities or damage to businesses. The independent study of the Genesis Advisers program and coaching processes mentioned previously yielded an assessed 1,400 percent ROI based on conservative salary assumptions. But beyond that, the following verbatim quotations from the study highlight the scope and dimensions of the potential impact of derailment or underperformance.[2]

- "In one business, under a struggling new leader, growth slowed by half in one region. When you look at the after-tax impact, that amounted to $7 to 8 M U.S."

- "Initiatives were not undertaken, and results were not met. A new product launch was delayed. When new product development problems arise, the impact of a poor transition could be $100 M U.S."

- "A key cost is loss of talent. There is a huge cost that goes beyond direct dollars. Hi-potentials are a scarce resource, and we're tough on them. If they don't make it, you've washed out a hi-potential."

Companies typically have systems in place to assess and manage other risks of comparable magnitude, and they should manage executive transition risk with equal rigor. An acceleration system is therefore an element of overall enterprise risk management.

Now consider the cumulative impact on performance of the many ongoing transitions occurring at all levels. Recall that about a quarter of all the leaders in typical *Fortune* 500 companies change jobs each year. Executives have even higher annual rates of transition—35 percent in the top three tiers of leadership in one study, with 22 percent moving internally and 13 percent being hired from the outside. And each transition materially impacts the performance of about a dozen people surrounding the leader—peers, direct reports, and bosses.

Imagine the value of accelerating all those transitions by only 10 percent, never mind 40 percent. Success in accelerating everyone contributes directly to improving company performance. It's even a potential source of competitive advantage; if you can help everyone get up to speed faster, the business will be more nimble and responsive. An acceleration system is therefore a key element of a high-performance organization.

Finally, think about what happens when your business goes through a significant change event—a restructuring, a phase of rapid growth, or integration of an acquisition. Every major change creates a ripple of individual transitions that cascades through the organization. The important "hard side" work of getting in place the right structure and systems and staffing the key positions is only the first phase of change implementation. To achieve planned objectives, such as acquisition synergy targets, strategic direction must be driven down through the organization; clarity about roles, responsibilities, and decision rights must be established; and relationship building must be accelerated.

The 90-day framework described in this book has been applied very successfully to accelerate the second phase of organizational change in Rapid Rewire implementations. The focus typically is on team acceleration, and it begins with the top team and flows down through the organization. Teams at every level use the same methodology, language, and tools to create 90-day plans and build relationships and teamwork. Success in applying this approach can make the difference between achieving targets and failing miserably. That's because, as many companies have learned painfully, the soft side of change is the hard side. An acceleration system is therefore an essential element of the organizational change management toolkit.

Whether the focus is on risk management, performance improvement, change implementation, or all three, companies have a big stake in accelerating transitions at every level—internally and externally, individually and organizationally. This means that they should manage leadership-transition acceleration as they would any critical business process—by putting in place the right framework, tools, and systems to accelerate everyone.

Given this, how should companies approach the design of acceleration systems? Following are ten design principles—guidelines you can apply to build the right solution for your business.

Identify the Critical Transitions

The starting point is to understand how many transitions are occurring in your organization and to focus first on accelerating the most important of them. It's surprising how many companies are unable to answer basic questions about the number of people who are being hired, getting promoted, moving between units, and making lateral moves. Without good data on the frequency of transitions—and, critically, without awareness of when they are occurring—it's difficult to design acceleration systems.

You need to understand transition frequencies in order to assess the costs and benefits of providing support at different levels and to efficiently allocate resources. Suppose, for example, that you anticipate a relatively high frequency of movement (greater than 30 percent) at the frontline leader level, perhaps because the business is growing rapidly. It's a good rule of thumb that leaders at this level should participate in transition workshops (in person or virtually) within their first 60 days on the job (in addition, as described later, to getting immediate launch resources at the time they move into their new roles). These workshops tend to work best with fifteen to twenty participants. You can use this information to plan where and when transition support will be offered.

Beyond knowing transition frequencies, it's valuable to know what the mix is of onboarding, inboarding (moves between units), promotion, and lateral moves. Knowing this allows you to tailor the support you're providing. That's because, as described later, support should be customized somewhat to the types of transitions leaders are experiencing.

Then you need to focus on critical transitions. Which are the most important transitions going on in your company? Suppose you're a small, rapidly growing pharmaceutical company. You have just received approval for a promising new drug; you're hiring a new sales force and need to get up to speed faster than a competitor. Your success in onboarding new salespeople may make the difference between great success and so-so performance. Your initial efforts therefore should focus on helping all those salespeople get up to speed as quickly as possible, as well as helping the sales organization as a whole to gel. Use the Transition Heat Map tool in figure 10-1 to summarize your assessments of which transitions are most critical in your organization.

FIGURE 10-1

Transition Heat Map

The Transition Heat Map is a tool for summarizing the most important transition acceleration priorities in your organization, as shown in the example below. Start by listing the key organizational units or groups or projects in the left-hand column. Then identify any major change events that are occurring in each of these units, groups, projects. Finally assess the relative intensity of key types of transitions—onboarding, promotion, geographic moves, and lateral moves—that are occurring in each organization. The result is a summary that you can use to communicate about priorities.

Organizational unit	Major change events	Transition intensity			
		Onboarding	Promotion	Geographic moves	Lateral moves
Unit A	Rapid growth	High	Low	High	Medium
Unit B	Turnaround	Medium	Low	Low	High
Unit C	Acquisition	None	Low	Medium	High

Identify Set-Up-to-Fail Dynamics

As discussed in the introduction, there are common traps new leaders fall into. Examples include staying in your comfort zone or trying to do too much too fast. These can largely be avoided through implementation of acceleration systems based on the principles discussed in this book.

However, there also are systematic mistakes that organizations make when putting leaders into new roles that need to be addressed in the design of acceleration systems.[3] Respondents to the HBR/IMD study highlighted classic ways that companies set up their leaders to fail. Reasons for unnecessary derailment or underperformance are summarized in table 10-1.

There is not much point in putting in place acceleration systems if your company is setting up leaders to fail in these ways. The implication is that you may need to address culture change as part of your broader effort to put a system in place. Suppose your company does a poor job of sizing the leaps that leaders are being asked to make. If it is, you may want to push for systematic use of the transition risk assessment discussed in the introduction. Likewise, if there are widespread problems with providing clarity about expectations, they can be addressed through disciplined use of the five conversations discussed in chapter 4.

Diagnose Existing Transition Support

Companies often have a patchwork quilt of existing systems for supporting transitions. One unit may do a good job of promoting lower-level leaders, another has an effective executive onboarding system, and yet another does a good job of supporting international moves. Because the benefits of having a companywide

TABLE 10-1

Reasons for transition failures

Reasons that apply to all transitions

- Insufficient clarity about expectations and mandates. Leaders are not given enough information, or conflicting information, about what they need to do to be successful.
- Not taking the STARS situation into account in hiring and promotion. Leaders are selected without enough attention being given to whether they're best suited for the challenges of the situation—for example, putting a person who is great at turnarounds in a sustaining-success or realignment situation.
- Pushing leaders to make leaps that are too big. Leaders are placed in new roles with very high levels of transition risk; they take on too much, and fail.
- Having a Darwinian leadership culture. Leaders are not provided with adequate support during transitions, perhaps because the culture misguidedly reinforces a sink-or-swim approach to leadership development.

Promotion-specific reasons	Onboarding-specific reasons (also applies to moves between units)
• People are promoted only because they're good at their current jobs. Leaders are not evaluated adequately on their ability to be effective at higher levels. • Training is provided too late or not at all. Leaders do not receive training (or receive it many months later) in the skills they need to be effective and so lose the opportunity to build credibility during their transitions. • Leaders are required to do their old jobs *and* their new ones. The company does a poor job of succession planning, causing newly promoted leaders to expend energy on their old roles at the most critical period in their new ones.	• Cultural fit is not taken into account in recruiting. Leaders are hired because they have certain capabilities, whether or not they're a good fit for the culture. • Support for cultural adaptation is not provided. Newly hired leaders are expected to figure out the culture on their own and make unnecessary early mistakes. • Support is not provided for identifying and connecting with key stakeholders. Newly hired leaders are expected to figure out on their own who will have influence over their success, and they don't make the right connections early enough.

acceleration system based on a common core framework are great, however, this mosaic of existing systems usually needs to be modified substantially or even replaced.

Before designing a companywide acceleration system, you must first make a thorough assessment of existing systems, as well as identify areas where no support is currently provided. To do this assessment, follow these guidelines:

- Identify and assess the status of your company's existing acceleration support frameworks and tools. What approaches have been used, and why? To what degree do they represent best practice?

- Examine the approaches (coaching programs, virtual workshops, self-guided materials) your organization currently uses to deliver transition support at all levels of the leadership pipeline. Evaluate the associated costs and benefits.

- Assess the overall coherence of your organization's approach to supporting different types of transitions—onboarding, promotion, and lateral and international moves. Is there a common core model for accelerating all transitions?

- Identify the key stakeholders (bosses, peers, direct reports, HR generalists, learning and development personnel) who do or could provide support during transitions.

- Assess the adequacy of your company's HR information systems (for example, websites) in directly supporting transitions and in providing the data about where and when transitions are occurring, so that you can provide support on a just-in-time basis.

Adopt a Common Core Model

Given the frequency with which people take on new jobs and the impact of each transition on others, it makes sense to have everyone—bosses, direct reports, and peers—employ the same common core model to support transition.

The foundation of an acceleration system is a unified, companywide framework, language, and toolkit for talking about and planning transitions. This probably is the single most important step your organization can take to build an acceleration system. Imagine that every leader in transition were able to converse with bosses, peers, and direct reports about the following:

- The STARS portfolio of challenges they had inherited—the mix of start-up, turnaround, accelerated growth, realignment, or sustaining success—and the associated challenges and opportunities

- Their technical, cultural, and political learning and the key elements of their learning plan

- Their progress in the five conversations—situation, expectations, style, resources, and progress—with their boss and direct reports

- Their agreed-upon priorities and plans for where they will secure early wins

- The alliances they need to build

A common core model makes discussions of these issues dramatically more efficient. Perhaps more importantly, it means that conversations will happen that wouldn't have happened otherwise. It also makes people more forthcoming, more likely to share confidences and information, and more tolerant of others' transition struggles. This kind of systematic support helps move the organization beyond sink or swim.

Deliver Support Just in Time

Transitions evolve through a series of predictable stages. New leaders begin their transitions with intensive diagnostic work. As they learn and gain increasing clarity about the situation, they shift to defining strategic direction (mission, goals, strategy, and vision) for their organizations. As the intended direction becomes clearer, they are better able to make decisions about key organizational issues—structure, processes, talent, and team. In tandem, they can identify opportunities to secure early wins and begin to drive the process of change.

The type of support that new leaders need, therefore, shifts in predictable ways as the transition process unfolds. Early on, support for accelerating learning—technical, cultural, and political—is key. As the leader's understanding grows, the focus of support should shift to helping him define strategic direction, lay the foundation for success, secure early wins, and so on.

Critically, leaders need to be offered transition support in digestible blocks. Once they are in their new roles, they are rapidly immersed in the flow of events and can devote only very limited time to learning, reflecting, and planning. If support is not delivered just in time, the new leader is not likely to use it.

A corollary is to leverage the time before entry to the maximum extent possible. Transitions begin with recruiting or selection, and not when leaders formally enter their new positions. This is a priceless period when new leaders can begin to learn about their organizations and plan their early days on the job.

Acceleration systems should therefore be designed to help new leaders get the maximum possible benefit from whatever preentry time is available to them. This means supporting new leaders' learning processes by providing them with key documents and tools that help them plan their early diagnostic activities, as well as helping them connect with key stakeholders as early as possible. For executives, it may be beneficial to have transition coaches engage in preentry diagnosis, including interviews with key stakeholders, and distill this knowledge into an actionable assessment that provides the basis for early discussions.

Use Structured Processes

The paradox of transition acceleration is that leaders in transition often feel too busy to learn and plan their transitions. They know they should be tapping into available resources and devoting time to planning their transitions, but the urgent demands of their new roles tend to crowd out this important work.

Although it helps to leverage the time before entry and to provide just-in-time support, transition processes also need to have action-forcing events. These include preset coaching meetings at each stage of the process or scheduled cohort events that take leaders out of the fray to engage in reflection and create or refine their 90-day plans.

The implication is that transition support should not be designed as a free-flowing process in which the leader sets the pace. It's better to create a series of focused events—coach meetings or cohort sessions—at critical stages. After undertaking preentry diagnosis of the situation and helping the leader engage in self-assessment, for example, the coach and client are well positioned to have a highly productive launch meeting to jump-start the process.

When transition coaching is provided, it's critical that the new leader and the coach connect early on in a focused and engaged way. One reason it can be beneficial for coaches to engage in intensive preentry diagnosis is that they have a precious resource—knowledge about the situation—that they can convey to the new leader. Their insight, offered in the critical early phases of the transition, can help cement the coach-client relationship.

Match Support to Transition Type

The 90-day framework and toolkit can be applied in all types of transition situations. However, the importance of different activities—for example, focusing more or less attention on learning about the culture—varies significantly, depending on the types of transitions leaders are experiencing. Therefore, it's often helpful to identify the most important types of transitions the company needs to support and to develop specific, targeted supplemental resources to support them.

In particular, there often are good reasons to provide new leaders with additional resources for dealing with two common types of transitions:

- **Promotion.** As discussed in chapter 1, when leaders are promoted they face a predictable set of challenges. The competencies required to be successful at the new level may be quite different from the skills that made them successful at their previous level. They also may be expected to play different roles, exhibit different behaviors, and engage with direct reports in different ways. So focused sets of resources should be provided that help newly promoted leaders understand what success looks like at the new level, assess themselves, and create a personal development plan.

- **Onboarding.** Likewise, when leaders join new organizations or move between units with distinct subcultures, they face major challenges in aligning expectations, adapting to new cultures, and building the right sorts of relationships. Focused, accessible resources for helping them understand what it takes to get things done and

assistance in identifying and connecting with key stakeholders can help reduce derailment and can speed time
to high performance.

Match Transition Support to Leader Level

If cost were not an issue, every transitioning leader would get
intensive, highly personalized support. In an ideal world, a
new leader would be assigned a transition coach who would
undertake an independent diagnosis and brief the person on
the results before entry. The coach would help the leader
engage in self-assessment and identify key transition risk factors. The coach also would help support diagnostic planning
and goal setting, assist with team assessment and alignment,
gather feedback on how the leader was doing, and, of course,
be available to the new leader as needed to talk through specific
issues.

Because the impact of executives on the business is great, it
often makes sense to provide them with transition coaching.
(If you do, be sure to understand that transition coaching is very
different from development coaching. See the box, "Transition Coaching and Developmental Coaching.") But it typically
doesn't make economic sense to provide it to leaders at lower
levels. The solution is threefold. First, identify alternative modes
for delivering transition support (for example, coaching versus
cohort sessions versus virtual workshops and self-guided materials). Second, assess the relative costs and benefits of the support, and third, match its delivery mode and extent to key levels
in the company's leadership pipeline in order to maximize the
return on investment.

Transition Coaching and Developmental Coaching

Transition coaching is very different from developmental coaching. It's essential that transition coaches have the business acumen necessary to act as trusted advisers to leaders in transition. In addition, a thorough knowledge of the organization and its culture is a prerequisite for effectiveness. For this reason, it can be dangerous for newly hired leaders to bring in their own coaches, as they may lack experience with transitions as well as an understanding of the culture and political system the leader is entering.

TABLE 10-2

Transition versus developmental coaching

Transition coaching	Developmental coaching

• Coach helps leader to
  – Assess both the business situation and himself in his new role
  – Create a strategy to build momentum
  – Create a strategy for managing himself
  – Develop an action plan
• Coach's business acumen ensures right mix of advice and behavioral coaching
	• Coach helps leader to
	  – Assess existing competencies and behaviors
	  – Identify gaps in competencies as well as dysfunctional behaviors
	  – Correct these challenges and build key competencies

Clarify Roles and Align Incentives

Transition support is a team sport. For any given new leader, typically there are many people who potentially can impact the success of the transition. Key players may include bosses, peers, direct reports, HR generalists, coaches, and mentors. Although primary responsibility for supporting a transition may be vested with one individual—typically a coach or HR generalist—it is important to think through the supportive roles that others could play and to identify ways to encourage them to do so.

A boss, for example, has an obvious stake in getting the new leader up to speed quickly but also may be dealing with other pressing demands. Careful thought must be given to providing bosses and other key players with guidelines and tools that allow them to be highly focused and efficient in supporting their new direct reports. HR generalists likewise can provide invaluable support to leaders who are onboarding by helping them navigate the new culture. But once again, they both need to know what to do and have incentives to do it.

Integrate with Other Talent Management Systems

Acceleration systems work best when they're linked with the company's recruiting and leadership development systems. This need for integration seems obvious on the face of it, because the best onboarding systems can't compensate for the sins of poor recruiting. If the company hires people who aren't likely to fit with the culture, then little can be done to reduce the risk of derailment through onboarding.

It's surprising, therefore, that many companies still do not do a good job of integrating recruiting and onboarding. Often, people in these functions report up through different parts of the organization and are led by people with different, perhaps even divergent, goals, measures of success, and incentives. A necessary first step is to have them under the same organizational umbrella and align their goals and incentives.

Beyond that, the company should think about transition risk when it engages in recruiting. Doing so means, as illustrated in figure 10-2, making transition risk tolerance part of the process of setting up searches. Often, businesses practice "best athlete" recruiting—hiring people because they have a needed set of capabilities and not paying enough attention to fit. It's fine to take a significant risk in bringing in someone from a very different culture, as long as you have been thoughtful about the trade-offs between individual capabilities and cultural fit, and as long as transition risk is explicitly evaluated during recruiting. Of course, doing this requires the company to have a good understanding of its culture and the reasons people might struggle to assimilate. This understanding can be refined, as illustrated in the figure, by feedback from successes and failures in onboarding.

There also is great value in feeding information about potential risks from recruiting to the onboarding process. Recruiting typically involves multiple forms of assessment, including psychometric instruments and in-depth interviews. The instruments

FIGURE 10-2

Linking recruiting and onboarding

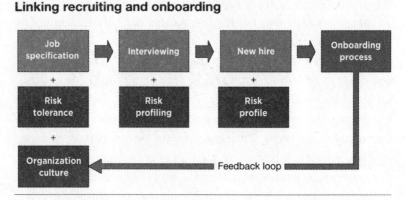

can provide transition coaches and workshop facilitators with valuable insight into leaders' styles and ways they might struggle in adapting to the culture. Interviews likewise can provide rich information about likely transition risks, as long as interviewers are explicitly asked to make assessments and develop a transition risk profile for new hires.

Then there is the relationship between leadership development systems and transition acceleration systems. Leadership development systems prepare talent to go to the next level. Transition acceleration systems should help them make the leap. Although this description makes the two seem distinct, in reality there are opportunities for connecting development and acceleration.

One example is including familiarization with the organization's core transition acceleration model in development programs. Doing so helps leaders take on a transition state of mind and think about how they will enter their next roles when the time comes. It also provides a foundation on which to build during the transition, a foundation that is valuable given the high demands that new leaders typically experience.

A second example is strengthening leadership development by assessing leaders' experience with different types of transitions using the STARS model. This model provides a basis for charting the progression of high-potential leaders through a series of positions that build their capability to manage a broad range of business situations. It also identifies potential development gaps—for example, that a leader has mostly managed turnarounds and needs to be channeled into experiences that provide exposure to a broader range of business situations.

To illustrate, think of your own job history. Take time to fill out the development grid, a tool for charting professional development shown in table 10-3.

TABLE 10-3

The development grid

The rows represent functions in which you have worked, and the columns represent types of business situations you have experienced. Chart every position you have held, plus any major project or task force assignments. For example, if your first job was in marketing in an organization (or unit) in the midst of a turnaround, place a circled 1 (indicating your first management position) in the corresponding cell of the matrix. If your next position was in sales in a new unit (or dealing with a new product or project)—a start-up situation—enter a circled 2 in that cell. If at the same time you were on a task force dealing with operations issues for the start-up, enter a 2 inside a triangle (indicating a project assignment) in the appropriate cell. Record all your jobs, and then connect the dots to illuminate your professional trajectory. Are there any blank columns or rows? What do they signify about your readiness for new positions? About your potential blind spots?

	Start-up	Turn-around	Accelerated growth	Realign-ment	Sustaining success
Marketing					
Sales					
Finance					
Human resources					
Operations					
R&D					
Information management					
Other					

Putting It All Together

Given the many transitions that occur in organizations and the substantial impact they have, it makes sense to evaluate the costs and benefits of designing and deploying companywide acceleration systems. Best-in-class systems are founded on a core transition acceleration framework and toolkit, provide support just in time, are customized to some degree for types of transitions, and are deployed in cost-effective ways throughout the organization. They also take the organizational context into account by aligning and incentivizing key stakeholders and by linking to recruiting and leadership development systems.

ACCELERATE EVERYONE—CHECKLIST

1. What are the most important transitions in your organization, and how often do they occur?

2. Is the organization able to identify where and when transitions are occurring?

3. Is there a common core transition acceleration framework, language, and toolkit?

4. Do leaders have the support they need, when they need it, and throughout their transitions? What could be done to provide focused resources for onboarding and promotion transitions?

5. Are the company's systems for recruiting and accelerating transitions linked in appropriate ways?

6. Should transition acceleration be part of your organization's curriculum for developing high-potential leaders?

7. How might the 90-day framework be used to accelerate organizational change—for example, restructuring or post-acquisition integration?

NOTES

PREFACE

1. I was aware of two exceptions: John J. Gabarro, *The Dynamics of Taking Charge* (Boston: Harvard Business School Press, 1987), and Linda Hill, *Becoming a Manager: How New Managers Master the Challenges of Leadership*, 2d ed. (Boston: Harvard Business School Press, 2003).

2. Dan Ciampa and Michael Watkins, *Right from the Start: Taking Charge in a New Leadership Role* (Boston: Harvard Business Press, 1999).

3. Michael Watkins, *Leadership Transitions Version 3.0* (Boston: Harvard Business Publishing, 2008). This e-learning product won the 2001 Brandon-Hill Excellence in E-Learning Silver Award in the performance-centered design category.

4. "Executive Onboarding: That Tricky First 100 Days," *The Economist*, July 13, 2006.

5. Michael Watkins, *Shaping the Game: The New Leader's Guide to Effective Negotiating* (Boston: Harvard Business School Press, 2006).

6. Peter H. Daly, Michael Watkins, and Cate Reavis, *The First 90 Days in Government: Critical Success Strategies for New Public Managers at All Levels* (Boston: Harvard Business School Press, 2006).

7. Michael Watkins, "The Pillars of Executive Onboarding," *Talent Management*, October 2008.

8. Michael Watkins, *Your Next Move: The Leader's Guide to Navigating Major Career Transitions* (Boston: Harvard Business Press, 2009).

9. Michael Watkins, "Picking the Right Transition Strategy," *Harvard Business Review*, January 2009, 47.

10. Michael Watkins, "How Managers Become Leaders: The Seven Seismic Shifts of Perspective and Responsibility," *Harvard Business Review*, June 2012, 65.

11. Excellent examples are Boris Groysberg and Robin Abrahams, "Five Ways to Bungle a Job Change," *Harvard Business Review*, January 2010, 137;

Keith Rollag, Salvatore Parise, and Rob Cross, "Getting New Hires Up to Speed Quickly," *Sloan Management Review*, January 15, 2005; and Jean-François Manzoni and Jean-Louis Barsoux, "New Leaders: Stop Downward Performance Spirals Before They Start," *HBR Blog Network*, January 16, 2009, http://blogs.hbr.org/hmu/2009/01/new-leaders-stop-downward-perf.html. Many surveys also have been done by executive recruiting companies, including some very solid research on the transition dimensions of CEO succession.

12. All these were introduced in the first edition of *The First 90 Days*.

13. See chapter 1: The Challenge, in Ciampa and Watkins, *Right from the Start*.

14. See the introduction to Watkins, *Your Next Move*.

INTRODUCTION

1. My survey of 1,350 HR leaders affiliated with the IMD business school, 2008, previously reported in Michael Watkins, *Your Next Move* (Boston, MA: Harvard Business Press, 2009).

2. Genesis Advisers, *Harvard Business Review*, and International Institute of Management Development, unpublished electronic survey, 2011.

3. My survey conducted in 2000 of senior HR executives at *Fortune* 500 companies, results previously reported in the first edition of *The First 90 Days*.

4. For each individual who transitions, there also are many others—direct reports, bosses, and peers—whose performance is negatively affected. In a 2009 survey of company presidents and CEOs, I asked for their best estimate of the number of people whose performance was significantly compromised by the arrival of a new midlevel manager. The average of the responses was 12.4 people.

5. My survey conducted in 2000 of senior HR executives at *Fortune* 500 companies, results previously reported in the first edition of *The First 90 Days*.

6. This research was conducted by two clients—a *Fortune* 100 health-care company and a *Fortune* 500 financial services company—of Genesis Advisers programs and coaching. Both used subjective estimates of improved performance and estimated ROI based on conservative salary cost criteria. The 2006 study by the global health-care company focused on 125 participants in transition programs or coaching. Program participants reported an average 38 percent improvement in performance, and coached executives reported an average 40 percent improvement. The estimated return on investment was 1,400 percent. The financial services company study conducted in 2008 focused

on assessing acceleration in time to break-even for 50 participants in a *First 90 Days* program. Participants reported an average 1.2-month decrease in time to break-even. ROI for the program was calculated to be roughly 300 percent based on salary costs only.

7. Michael Watkins survey of participants in two Harvard Business School General Management Program (GMP) cohorts, 2010 and 2011, unpublished study.

CHAPTER 1

1. Survey of 1,350 HR leaders affiliated with the IMD business school, 2008, previously reported in Michael Watkins, *Your Next Move: The Leader's Guide to Navigating Major Career Transitions* (Boston: Harvard Business Press, 2009). See also Boris Groysberg, Andrew N. McLean, and Nitin Nohria, "Are Leaders Portable?" *Harvard Business Review* (May 2006): 92–100.

2. Michael Watkins, *Your Next Move: The Leader's Guide to Navigating Major Career Transitions* (Boston: Harvard Business Press, 2009).

3. The original quotation is, "I suppose it is tempting, if the only tool you have is a hammer, to treat everything as if it were a nail." Abraham Maslow, *The Psychology of Science: A Reconnaissance* (New York: Harper Collins, 1966), 15.

CHAPTER 2

1. N. M. Tichy and M. A. Devanna, *The Transformational Leader* (New York: John Wiley & Sons, 1986).

CHAPTER 5

1. For an early discussion of the importance of early wins, see Dan Ciampa and Michael Watkins, *Right from the Start: Taking Charge in a New Leadership Role* (Boston: Harvard Business School Press, 1999), chapter 2.

2. See John J. Gabarro, *The Dynamics of Taking Charge* (Boston: Harvard Business School Press, 1987).

3. See wikipedia.org/wiki/Confirmation_bias.

4. George Will, "Price of Safety Sometimes Paid in Technology-Boosted War," *Washington Post*, June 12, 1994.

5. My colleague Amy Edmondson developed this very useful distinction.

6. See Michael Watkins and Max Bazerman, "Predictable Surprises: The Disasters You Should Have Seen Coming," *Harvard Business Review* (March 2003): 5–12.

CHAPTER 6

1. This is an adaptation of the McKinsey "7-S" organizational analysis framework. See R. H. Waterman, T. J. Peters, and J. R. Phillips, "Structure Is Not Organization," *Business Horizons*, 1980. For an overview, see Jeffrey L. Bradach, "Organizational Alignment: The 7-S Model," Case 9-497-045 (Boston: Harvard Business School, 1996). The seven S's are strategy, structure, systems, staffing, skills, style, and shared values.

2. See wikipedia.org/wiki/SWOT_analysis. For an early description of SWOT, see Edmund P. Learned, C. Roland Christiansen, Kenneth Andrews, and William D. Guth, *Business Policy: Text and Cases* (Homewood, IL: Irwin, 1969).

3. Building "ambidextrous" organizations that can do both of these well is a challenge. See Michael L. Tushman and Charles O'Reilly III, *Winning Through Innovation: A Practical Guide to Leading Organizational Change and Renewal*, rev. ed. (Boston: Harvard Business School Press, 2002).

CHAPTER 7

1. For a discussion of types of players, see T. DeLong and V. Vijayaraghavan, "Let's Hear It For B Players," *Harvard Business Review* (June 2003): 96–102, 137.

2. M. Huselid, R. Beatty, and B. Becker, "'A Players' or 'A Positions'? The Strategic Logic of Workforce Management," *Harvard Business Review* (December 2005): 110–117, 154.

3. See, for example, A. Edmondson, M. Roberto, and M. Watkins, "A Dynamic Model of Top Management Team Effectiveness: Managing Unstructured Task Streams," *Leadership Quarterly* 14, no. 3 (Spring 2003): 297–325.

4. For a discussion of the importance of perceptions of fairness in group process, see W. Chan Kim and Renée A. Mauborgne, "Fair Process: Managing in the Knowledge Economy," *Harvard Business Review* (July–August 1997): 127–136.

CHAPTER 8

1. David Lax and Jim Sebenius coined this term. "Thinking Coalitionally," in *Negotiation Analysis*, ed. H. Peyton Young (Ann Arbor: University of Michigan Press, 1991).

2. See D. Krackhardt and J. R. Hanson, "Informal Networks: The Company Behind the Chart," *Harvard Business Review* (July–August 1993).

3. See the seminal work on human motivation by David McClelland. *Human Motivation* (Cambridge: Cambridge University Press, 1988).

4. See L. Ross and R. Nisbett, *The Person and the Situation: Perspectives of Social Psychology*, 2d ed. (London: Pinter & Martin, 2011).

5. Aristotle, *The Art of Rhetoric*, trans. H. Lawson-Tancred (New York: Penguin Classics, 1992).

6. See James Sebenius, "Sequencing to Build Coalitions: With Whom Should I Talk First?" in *Wise Choices: Decisions, Games, and Negotiations*, ed. Richard J. Zeckhauser, Ralph L. Keeney, and James K. Sebenius (Boston: Harvard Business School Press, 1996).

CHAPTER 9

1. See Ronald Heifetz, *Leadership Without Easy Answers* (Cambridge, MA: Belknap Press, 1994), 251.

2. This was originally developed as a model of anxiety. See R. M. Yerkes and J. D. Dodson, "The Relation of Strength of Stimulus to Rapidity of Habit Formation," *Journal of Comparative Neurology and Psychology* 18 (1908): 459–482. Naturally, this model has limitations and is most useful as a metaphor. For a discussion of limitations, see "How Useful Is the Human Function Curve?" www.trance.dircon.co.uk/curve.html.

3. For a discussion of going to the balcony in the context of negotiation, see chapter 1 of William Ury, *Getting Past No: Negotiating Your Way from Confrontation to Cooperation* (New York: Bantam Doubleday, 1993).

CHAPTER 10

1. Independent study by *Fortune* 100 global health-care company focused on 125 participants in Genesis Advisers transition programs or coaching. Program participants reported an average 38 percent improvement in performance, and coached executives reported an average 40 percent improvement.

2. Direct quotations taken from the same study of Genesis Advisers programs and coaching processes.

3. For a wonderful discussion of set-up-to-fail dynamics, see J. Manzoni and J. L. Barsoux, *The Set-Up-To-Fail Syndrome: Overcoming the Undertow of Expectations* (Boston: Harvard Business Press, 2007).

INDEX

accelerated-growth situations, 72, 73.
  See also STARS model
  organizational psychology in, 74–75
  resource needs in, 101
  rewarding success in, 83–84
  support needed in, 97
acceleration, 239–257
  of alignment, 164
  alliances and, 219–220
  checklists for, 16–17, 42–43, 67,
      86, 112–113, 164, 197–198,
      219–220, 237, 257
  common core model for, 246–247
  critical transitions and, 242–243
  designing systems for, 242
  for everyone, 12
  just-in-time support for, 248–249
  of learning, 45–67
  role clarification and, 252–253
  self-management and, 237
  structured processes in, 249
  of teams, 197–198
  value of, 239–242
accessibility, 125
accountability, 157
actionable insights, 49–50

action-forcing events, 219
action imperative, 5, 48–49, 193
action planning, 92
adequacy, 150–152
adversaries, 208–211
advice and counsel, 38, 39–40,
      234–236
advisers, 38, 39–40, 234–236
alignment, 11, 139–164
  adequacy and, 150–152
  adversaries and, 210
  checklist on, 164
  coherence and, 149–150
  common pitfalls in, 141–143
  diagnosing problems in,
      145–146
  of expectations, 29–30, 34
  getting started with, 146–148
  organizational architects and,
      140–141
  organizational architecture and,
      143–145, 163
  skill bases and, 162–163
  of teams, 182–189
  testing strategic, 64
  trade-offs in, 156–157

alliances, 199–200
  acceleration system design and, 247
  checklist on, 219–220
  of convenience, 208–209
  defining objectives for, 202–203
  influence diagrams and, 207–208
  influence networks and, 204–206
  influence strategies and, 213–219
  pivotal people in, 211–213
  supporters, opponents, persuadables
    and, 208–211
  understanding influence landscape
    and, 203–211
  winning and blocking, 204
alternatives, 212–213
ambiguity, 100
analysts, outside, 56
answers, premature, 6, 49
app, First 90 Days, 16
architecture, organizational, 140–141,
    143–145, 163, 169–170
Aristotle, 214
assumptions
  about teams, 172–173
  cultural differences in, 31, 33
authority, 22–23, 124, 154
autonomy, 89
awareness, 132–133

backsliding, 42
balance, 12, 21–22
barriers, 53
behavior
  changing, 119–120, 130–131,
    134–135
  dysfunctional, 225–226

Belenko, Alexia, 199–201
benchmarks, 133
blocking alliances, 204
boundaries, undefended, 225
break-even point, 3–5
  actionable insights and, 49–50
  definition of, 3
breakpoints, 35
brittleness, 225
burning platforms, 4, 73
business orientation, 28–29, 34
buy-in, 109–110, 213–214

capability analysis, 151
capital, 149
career paths, 255–256
  conversations about, 95, 106–107
  networks and, 39–40
  number of transitions in, 2–3
Cates, Vaughan, 87–88
challenges, 53
  awareness of, evaluating, 65
  diagnosing, 59
  in promotions, 25
  STARS model and, 83, 84
change
  agents of, 130
  behavioral, identifying and
    supporting, 119–120
  capacity to absorb, 142–143
  for change's sake, 141
  creating momentum in, 7–8
  history of, learning about, 52
  leading, 76–80, 132–136
  matching strategy to type of,
    69–86

planned, collective learning versus, 132–134
STARS model of, 71–75
traps in, 5–6
waves of, 117–118
checklists, 257
acceleration, 16–17, 42–43, 138
on alignment, 164
on alliances, 219–220
on communicating with bosses, 91
on early wins, 138
FOGLAMP, 131
on learning, 67
on negotiating success, 112–113
off-site planning, 188–189
onboarding, 34
on self-management, 237
on strategy and situation, 86
on teams, 197–198
Chen, Michael, 87–88
choice-shaping, 216
coaching, 249, 251–252
coalitions, 11, 206
coherence, 149–150
commitment, 187, 230
common core model, 246–247
communication
of bad news, 90
with bosses, 90
early wins and, 126–127
formality of, 23–24
influence networks and, 205–206
informal networks and, 28
promotions and, 23–24
shared language in, 30–31
structured learning methods and, 57–60
style preferences in, 94–95, 104
in virtual teams, 196
of vision, 185–188
when working at a distance, 108–109
competencies, 9
alignment and, 145, 146, 149
identifying sources on, 54–57
problem preferences and, 35–38
relearning to learn and, 38–39
sticking with what you know, 5, 20
for strategy implementation, 153
in teams, 171
complexity, in organizational structure, 142
concessions, 212
conclusions, premature, 6, 49
confirmation bias, 123
conflict
cultural norms of, 32
engaging with, 126–127
style conversations and, 105–106
consensus building, 11, 192–195
consult-and-decide process, 192–195
consultation, 213–214
context, 257
control, need for, 225
conversations
acceleration system design and, 247
with the boss, 93–96
on expectations, 94, 98–100
on personal development, 95, 106–107
on resources, 94, 100–103
situational diagnosis, 93–94, 96–97
on style, 94–95, 103–106
with teams, 110–112

core processes, 145–146
  alignment of, 157–161
  evaluating, 160
  improving, 160–161
credibility, 7, 8
  early wins and, 10, 124–126
  resource conversations and, 101–102
cultural interpreters, 234–236
cultural problems, 37
culture
  adapting to, 30–33, 34
  behavior changes and, 134–135
  changing architecture to change, 163
  definition of, 30
  differences in work, 28
  early wins and, 121, 122
  help with, 41
  "inboarding" and, 33
  learning about, 49, 53, 66
  onboarding and, 25–27, 30–33
  organization history and, 48
  STARS framework and, 83–85
  symbols in, 30
customers, 55, 137, 148

decision diffusion, 192
decision making, 7–8
  analysis of past, 62
  avoiding, 226
  balance and, 12
  boundaries in, 104–105
  employee scope of, 156
  fairness in, 194–195
  implementation-dependent, 169
  influence landscape and,
      203–211

pivotal people in, 211–213
politics of, 22–23
problem preferences and, 35–38
promotions and, 22–23
rights in, 154, 155
in teams, 191–195
defensiveness, 39, 225
delegation, 22
denial, 39, 74, 133
design, organizational, 143–145
development coaching, 251–252
development grids, 255–256
diagnosis
  of change situations, 71–75
  direct reports and, 58–60
  of existing transition support,
      244–246
  leading change and, 132–133
  for managing change, 133–134
  of misalignments, 145–146
  situational, conversation on,
      93–94, 96–97
  skills in, 47
  STARS portfolio, 75–76, 77
  structured learning methods and,
      61–62
  SWOT analysis in, 60, 63
  time lines for, 92
  of your boss's style, 103–104
direct reports
  learning from, 66
  one-on-one meetings with,
      58–60, 64
discipline, 120, 227, 229–231
distributors, 55–56
Dura Corporation, 45–47
dysfunctional behaviors, 225–226

Eiklid, Rolf, 201
embedded knowledge, 162
emotional escalation, 230
employee satisfaction surveys, 61
Energix, 25–27
energy levels, 171
engagement, 126–127
environment, business, 28–29, 137
Erikson, Stephen, 221–223
ethos, 214
evaluation, 2, 29
    of 90-day plans, 109–110
    of advice-and-counsel networks, 235
    for early wins, 128, 130
    in recruiting, 254–255
    self-, 228
    STARS framework and, 83–85
    of teams, 170–178
excellence
    promotions and, 21
expectations
    alignment of, 29–30, 34
    clarity about, 100
    conversations about, 94, 98–100
    managing, 92
    with multiple bosses, 107–108
    negotiating clear, 40–41
    negotiating success and, 87–113
    resource conversation and, 100–103
    setting unrealistic, 6
    underpromising and, 99–100
expertise, 162, 173, 206

facilitators, transition, 60
family life, 231–233
fear, 39

feedback, 229
    learning from, 65
    personal development and, 107
First 90 Days App, 16
focus
    behavioral change and, 120
    credibility and, 126
    diagnosing, 59
    early wins and, 124
    learning and, 47
    in self-management, 229–230
    in teams, 171
    on wrong type of learning, 6
focus groups, 61
FOGLAMP checklist, 131
framing, 214–215
functional expertise, 173

Geffen, Liam, 165–166
General Electric (GE), 60
Genesis Advisers, 2, 5–6
Global Foods, 69–70
goals. *See also* milestones
    in 90-day plans, 109–110
    alignment of, 146, 158
    alliances and, 202–203
    break-even point, 3–5
    delegation and, 22
    early wins and, 98, 117–121, 130
    in leading change, 77–78
    learning plan, 63–65
    resource conversation and, 100–103
    style differences and, 105–106
    for teams, 183
    translating into responsibilities, 22
    virtuous cycles and, 8

golden rule of transitions, 110–111
Gould, Julia, 19–21
group dynamics, 178
growth, accelerated, 71, 72, 73

Hadley, Chris, 45–47
Harvard Business Review, 2, 5–6, 83
heat maps, transition, 243
hero leaders, 81–83
hidden transitions, 3
human resources, 246

implementation assessment,
    152–153
"inboarding," 33
    frequency of transitions, 243
incentive equation, 184–185
incentives, 139–140, 155
    alignment of, 156–157, 252–253
    for teams, 183–185
incrementalism, 217–218
influence
    cultural norms of, 32
    defining objectives for, 202–203
    diagrams of, 207–208
    networks, mapping, 204–206
    promotions and, 22–23
    strategies, crafting, 213–219
    understanding landscape of,
        203–211
information silos, 136
initiatives
    attempting too much with, 6
innovation, 120
insights, actionable, 49–50

integration
    cross-functional, 153, 154
    with talent management systems,
        253–256
integrators, 56–57, 65
interfaces, key, 64, 65
International Institute of Management
    Development, 2, 5–6
interpersonal learning, 54
interviews, 61
isolation, 226

Jaffey, Hannah, 139–140
Jones, David, 25–27
judgment, 171, 177–178

key performance indicators, 173

language differences, 30–31, 186
lateral moves, 243
leaders
    assimilating at GE, 60
    characteristics of credible,
        125–126
    credibility of, 124–126
    criticizing previous, 167
    of former peers, 123–124
    hero versus steward, 81–83
    leading change and, 76–80
    matching change strategy to
        situation, 69–86
    number of transitions in career, 2–3
    organizational architecture and,
        143–145

presence of, 24
self-management by, 81–83
set-up-to-fail dynamics and, 244, 245
styles of, 81–83, 91
teams and, 189–196
transition support and level of, 251–252
leadership development, 255
learning
accelerating, 10, 45–67
acceleration system design and, 247
action imperative and, 48–49
agenda for, 50–54, 63
in change efforts, 118
checklist on, 67
collective, planned change versus, 132–134
credibility and, 127
early wins and, 130
educating the boss and, 99
external sources for, 54–56
focused, 78
getting help with, 66
guiding questions for, 51–54
identifying sources for, 54–57
internal sources for, 54, 56–57
as investment, 49–50
planning for, 48
plans, creating, 63–65
from process analysis, 161
relearning how to learn and, 38–39
roadblocks to, 47–49
structured methods for, 57–63
technical, 54
wrong type of, focus on, 6
Lee, Elena, 115–116
Lewin, Karl, 69–70, 77, 78–79

listening, active, 213–214
logos, 214
low-hanging fruit trap, 118–119
loyalty, 206

manipulation, 121
marketing, self, 125
market tours, 62
Maslow, Abraham, 38
MedDev, 199–201
meetings
cultural norms of, 32
off-site, 188–189
one-on-one, with direct reports, 58–60, 64
metaknowledge, 162
metrics, 22, 79, 153
alignment of, 156–157, 158–159, 163
for teams, 183
milestones, 13, 15–16
mission, 146, 148
momentum, 7–8
early wins and, 10
motivation, 182–183, 185, 211
mythology, company, 57, 127–128

negotiating success, 10–11, 87–113
checklist for, 112–113
definition of, 88
expectations conversation and, 98–100
focus on the fundamentals in, 90–93
with multiple bosses, 107–108

negotiating success (*continued*)
   personal development conversation
      and, 106–107
   planning conversations in, 93–96
   resource conversation in, 100–103
   situational diagnosis and, 95–97
   style conversation in, 103–106
   working at a distance and, 108–109
negotiation, for resources, 102–103
networks and networking
   advice-and-counsel, 39–40, 234–236
   influence, mapping, 204–206
   informal communication and, 28
   reworking, 39–40
90-day plans, 13, 15–16
   building consensus on, 11
   negotiating, 109–110
norms, 31, 32
   resource conversations and, 102
   for virtual teams, 196

off-site meetings, 188–189
onboarding, 12, 24–33
   breakpoints in, 35
   business orientation and, 28–29
   checklists for, 34, 42–43
   culture differences and, 25–27
   expectations alignment and, 29–30
   frequency of transitions, 243
   help for, 41
   integration of recruiting and,
      253–255
   people who want to hold you back
      and, 40–41
   pillars of effective, 28
   preparing yourself for, 33–41

reasons for failures in, 245
   stakeholder connections and, 29
   support for, 250–251
   vulnerabilities assessment for, 35–38
open systems, 143–144
operating models, 29
opponents, 208–211
opportunities, 53, 59, 65
organizational architects, 140–141
organizational architecture. *See*
   architecture, organizational
organizational climate surveys, 61
organizational history, 48, 75
organizational psychology, 74–75
organizational structure. *See* structure,
   organizational

pathos, 214
performance
   credibility and, 125
   evaluating, 29
   linking resource conversations to,
      102, 103
   questions about, 51–52
   strategy and situation type and, 79
   stress and, 226–227
   transitions' impact on, 239–240
personal development conversations,
   95, 106–107
personal disciplines, 227, 229–231
personality, 212
personal life, 231–233
perspective, 21–22
persuadables, 208–211
persuasion
   choice-shaping in, 216

consultation in, 213–214
  framing in, 214–215
  incrementalism in, 217–218
  sequencing in, 218–219
  social influence and, 216–217
Phoenix Systems, 45–47
pilot projects, 62
pivotal people, 211–213
planning
  action, 92
  for learning, 48
  in negotiating success, 93–96
  off-site, 188–189
  project planning template,
    130–131
  time for, 229
plant tours, 62
platforms, burning, 4, 73
political counselors, 234–236
political problems, 37
politics
  accelerated growth and, 73–74
  counselors on, 39–40
  decision making and, 22–23
  early wins and, 137
  identifying sources on, 54–57
  learning about, 54
  shadow organization and, 54
power. *See also* influence
  coalitions, 206
  influence networks and, 204–206
  sources of, 206
preparation, 9–10, 19–43
  for onboarding, 33–41
  for promotions, 21–24
presence, 24
priorities, early wins and, 119

problems
  communicating to bosses, 90–91
  early wins and, 118–121, 136–138
  preferences on types of, 35–38
processes
  alignment of, 145–146, 147, 157–161
  alignment of, with structure,
    159–160
  analysis of, 62, 158–159
  bottlenecks in, 158–159
  core, 145–146, 157–161
  delegation and, 22
  learning agenda on, 52
  onboarding, 41
  structured, in acceleration
    systems, 249
  team, 190–191
process maps, 160–161
procurement, 56
productivity, 160
professional development, 255–256
project planning template, 130–131
promotions, 12
  challenges in, 25
  communication and, 23–24
  cultural norms on, 32
  delegating and, 22
  frequency of transitions, 243
  influencing others and, 22–23
  leadership presence and, 24
  onboarding, 24–33
  perspective and, 21–22
  preparing yourself for, 21–24
  reasons for failures in, 245
  support for, 250
proprietary areas, 99
psychology, organizational, 74–75

pull tools, 182–183
push tools, 182–183

quality, 160
quitting, 231

Rapid Rewire implementations, 241
realignments, 72, 73, 74.
    See also STARS model
    behavior change and, 135–136
    leadership style and, 81
    leading change and, 133
    leading change in, 79–80
    organizational psychology in, 75
    resistance to, 82
    resource needs in, 101, 102
    rewarding success in, 83–84, 85
    support needed in, 97
reciprocity, 217
recruiting, 253–255
reflection, structured, 223–224, 230–231
relational knowledge, 162
relationships. *See also* alliances
    with bosses, 10–11, 87–93
    conversations with the boss and,
        93–96
    with former peers, 123–124
    horizontal, neglecting, 6
    with people who want to hold you
        back, 40–41
    with stakeholders, 29
    in teams, 171
reliability, 160
reporting relationships
    accountability and, 157

    alignment of work effort and, 155
    structure and, 154
reputation, 123, 217
research and development, 56
resistance, 82, 133, 209–210
resources, 53
    access to, as source of power, 206
    alignment and, 149
    conversations about, 94, 100–103
    negotiating for, 102–103
    skill bases, 162–163
respect, 181
restructuring, 142
reward systems, 139–140
    alignment of, 155, 156–157,
        158–159
    cultural norms of, 32
    individual versus collective
        performance in, 183–185
    STARS framework and, 83–85
    for teams, 183–185
rhetoric, 214
risk assessment, 12–13, 14
    for early wins, 128, 130
    recruiting and, 254–255
    of transitions, 239–240
rites of passage, 124
role transitions, 1
    clarification of, 252–253
    letting go of the past in, 19–20
    promotions, 21–24

sales departments, 56
self-discipline, 38
self-management, 81–83, 221–237
    90-day strategies in, 227, 228

checklist for, 237
dysfunctional behaviors and,
225–226
pillars of, 227–236
staying on track with, 236–237
taking stock in, 223–224
sequencing, 218–219
set-up-to-fail dynamics, 244, 245
shadow organizations, 54
situational diagnosis conversations,
93–94, 96–97
situational pressures, 211–212
skill bases, 145, 146
developing, 162–163
identifying gaps and resources in,
162–163
social dynamics, 78
social influence, 216–217
solutions, premature, 6, 49
staff, 56
helping with transitions, 110–111
stakeholders, 246
identifying and connecting with
key, 41
influence networks and, 205–206
relationships with, 29, 34
Stanford Research Institute (SRI), 151
STARS model, 71–75. See also
start-ups; turnarounds
acceleration system design and, 247
alignment and, 142
behavior change and, 135–136
challenges in and preferences for,
83, 84
decision making and, 194
early wins and, 122
expectations based on, 98

leadership development and, 255
leadership styles and, 81–83
leading change and, 132
portfolio diagnosis for, 75–76, 77
requirements of bosses in, 89
resources conversation and,
100–103
rewarding success and, 83–85
situational diagnosis conversation
and, 93–94, 96–97
strategic direction and, 153–154
teams and, 174, 182–183
start-ups, 9, 10, 71–72. See also STARS
model
organizational psychology in, 74
resource needs in, 101
rewarding success in, 83–84
support needed in, 97
steward leaders, 81–83
sticking with what you know, 5, 20
vulnerabilities assessment and,
35–38
storytelling, 127–128, 187
persuasion and, 214–215
strategy
alignment of, 145–146, 147,
148–154
communicating, 23–24
early wins and, 137
identifying sources on, 54–57
implementation assessment,
152–153
leading change in, 76–80
matching to situation, 9, 10, 69–86
modifying direction of, 153–154
organizational architecture and, 144
testing alignment with, 64

strengths, 38. *See also* sticking with
    what you know
stress, 39, 40, 226–227
structure, organizational, 139–140,
    144–145, 154–157
  alignment and, 146
  assessing, 155
  complexity in, 142
  elements of, 154–155
  influence networks and, 205–206
  process alignment with, 159–160
  shaping, 154–157
  trade-offs in, 156–157
structured reflection, 223–224
style
  conversation with boss on, 94–95,
    103–106
  diagnosing your boss's, 103–104
  leadership, 81–83, 91
success
  celebrating team, 196
  negotiating, 10–11, 87–113
  rewarding, 83–85
  strategies for, 227, 228
suppliers, 55
support, 54, 132–133, 201–202, 227
  building systems for, 231–236
  just-in-time, 248–249
  for transitions, existing, 244–246
  transition type and, 250–251
  in waves of change, 118
supporters, 208–211
sustaining success, 72, 73, 74.
    See also STARS model
  organizational psychology in, 75
  resource needs in, 101

rewarding success in, 85
support needed in, 97
SWOT (strengths, weaknesses, oppor-
    tunities, threats) analysis, 60, 63,
    150, 151–152
symbols, cultural, 30, 124, 127–128, 210

talent management, 29, 253–256
teachable moments, 128
teams and team building, 11, 38,
    165–198
  alignment of, 168, 182–189
  assessment of, 170–178
  assumptions about, 172–173
  backups for, 181
  buy-in from, 169
  categorizing members of, 179–181
  checklist on, 197–198
  common traps in, 167–170
  criticality of positions in, 174–175
  decision making in, 191–195
  delegation and, 22
  evolving, 179–181
  five conversations with, 110–112
  functional expertise and, 173
  goals and metrics for, 183
  group dynamics in, 178
  incentives for, 183–185
  judgment in, 171, 177–178
  leadership in, 78–79
  leadership style and, 82–83
  leading, 189–196
  off-site meetings of, 188–189
  replacement decisions about, 180–181
  respect in, 181

retaining good people in, 168–169
stability versus change in, 168
STARS mix and, 174
teamwork and, 173–174
virtual, 195–196
vision articulation for, 185–188
when to change, 167–168
technical advisers, 234–236
technical learning, 54
technical problems, 37
threshold issues, 171–172
timeliness, 160
transitions
  benefits of, 2
  break-even point in, 3–5
  causes of failure in, 9
  coaching for, 249, 251–252
  critical, identifying, 242–243
  criticality of, 1
  diagnosing types of, 12–13, 14
  existing support for, diagnosing,
     244–246
  facilitators for, 60
  golden rule of, 110–111
  heat maps of, 243
  hidden, 3
  impact of, on companies, 239–240,
     242
  milestones in, 13, 15–16
  multiple or parallel, 13
  number of, in a career, 2–3
  of others, impact of, 3
  preparing for, 9–10, 19–43
  reasons for failure in, 245
  risk assessment and, 12–13, 14
  traps in, 5–6

type of, support and, 250–251
trust, 7, 8
  in teams, 171
  working at a distance and, 108–109
turnarounds, 9, 10, 72–73.
  See also STARS model
  behavior change and, 135–136
  leadership style and, 81
  leading change and, 132–133
  leading change in, 79–80
  organizational psychology in, 74
  resource needs in, 101, 102
  support needed in, 97

untouchables, 99
urgency, sense of, 74, 120

value
  of accelerating transitions,
     240–241
  break-even point in, 3–5, 49–50
values, 32, 125. *See also* norms
vicious cycles, 1
  virtuous cycles versus, 7–8
virtuous cycles, 7–8
  learning agendas and, 50–51
vision, 132–133, 148
  articulating to teams, 185–188
  attributes of inspiring, 185–186
  commitment to, 187
  communicating, 23–24
  inspirations for, 186
  learning agenda and, 52
vulnerabilities, assessing, 35–38

winning alliances, 204
wins, early, 10, 115–138
    alliances and, 202–203
    avoiding predictable surprises in,
        136–138
    behavioral changes and, 119–120,
        134–135
    business priorities for, 119
    checklist on, 138
    communication and, 126–127
    credibility and, 124–126
    evaluation tool for, 128, 130
    expectations conversations on, 98
    FOGLAMP checklist for, 131
    identifying, 122–131
    importance of, to the boss, 92–93
    launching projects for, 128–131
    in leading change, 77–78
    leading change and, 132–136
    learning agenda and, 53
    learning priorities and, 66
    leveraging, 130–131
    principles for, 121–122
    reputation and, 123
    situation type and, 79
    storytelling and, 127–128
    waves of, 117–118
work avoidance, 226
work-flow maps, 160–161

Yerkes-Dodson curve, 226–227

ABOUT THE AUTHOR

MICHAEL D. WATKINS is the world's leading expert on accelerating transitions and a cofounder of Genesis Advisers (www.genesisadvisers.com), a leadership development consultancy that specializes in the design of onboarding and transition acceleration solutions, workshops, and coaching for *Fortune* 500 companies. He is also a professor of leadership at the IMD business school in Lausanne, Switzerland, where he teaches in the school's senior executive programs. Previously he was a professor at the Harvard Business School and the Harvard Kennedy School of Government.

Professor Watkins's passion is helping executives take charge effectively, lead their teams, and transform their organizations.

In addition to *The First 90 Days*, Professor Watkins is the author or coauthor of dozens of articles and books on leadership and transitions. Recent publications include: "How Managers Become Leaders" (*Harvard Business Review*, June 2012); *Your Next Move: The Leader's Guide to Navigating Major Career Transitions* (Harvard Business Press, 2009); and "Picking the Right Transition Strategy" (*Harvard Business Review*, January 2009).

A native of Canada, Professor Watkins received his undergraduate degree in electrical engineering from the University of Waterloo, did graduate work in law and business at the University of Western Ontario, and completed his PhD in decision sciences at Harvard University.